The Author vs. Editor Dilemma

The **Leadership Secret** to Unlocking Your Team, Your Time, and Your Impact

Brandon M. Smith

Copyright © 2022, Brandon M. Smith

All rights reserved. No part of this book may be used or reproduced by any means, graphic, electronic, or mechanical (including any information storage retrieval system) without the express written permission from the author, except in the case of brief quotations for use in articles and reviews wherein appropriate attribution of the source is made.

Publishing support provided by
Ignite Press
5070 N. Sixth St. #189
Fresno, CA 93710
www.IgnitePress.us

ISBN: 979-8-9860848-0-0
ISBN: 979-8-9860848-1-7 (Hardcover)
ISBN: 979-8-9860848-2-4 (E-book)
ISBN: 979-8-9860848-3-1 (Audiobook)

For bulk purchase and for booking, contact:

Brandon Mikel Smith
brandon@theworkplacetherapist.com

Because of the dynamic nature of the Internet, web addresses or links contained in this book may have been changed since publication and may no longer be valid. The content of this book and all expressed opinions are those of the author and do not reflect the publisher or the publishing team. The author is solely responsible for all content included herein.

Library of Congress Control Number: 2022905594

Cover design by Agus BudiYono
Edited by Charlie Wormhoudt
Interior design by Jetlaunch

FIRST EDITION

Acknowledgments

I've come to believe that every book takes a different journey from idea to reality. This book has been no different. And as with any journey, there have been many companions along the way who offered me a word of encouragement, a valuable critique, a vote of confidence, companionship, and, most importantly, the gift of their most precious resource—their time.

To my editorial board, thank yous will never fully honor the time, advice, and counsel that you provided. Cathy Fyock, Emily Smith, Whitney Mendoza, and Robert Sawyer you all gave time, attention, care, and perspectives that not only forced me to re-examine the book but also forced me to re-examine my voice. As a result, this book became a better book, and I became a better Author.

To Cathy Fyock, book coach extraordinaire, the book wouldn't have happened if you had not provided me the guidance, structure, and accountability that I so desperately needed. You provided just the right amount of Editing and coaching as I Authored my way through this journey. And you even added a little hot sauce along the way.

To Everett O'Keefe and the team at Ignite Press, thank you for your guidance, prompting, cajoling, and encouragement to help me take this project over the finish line. Your work took a manuscript and made it into something I, and others, can touch and hold. For that, I will be eternally grateful.

To all my clients, thank you for sharing with me the intimate details of your lives. Without that gift, I would never be able to not only see the need for this book but also tell the real stories that are woven through this book. I hope that your stories of struggle and inspiration can be a gift to all of those who read this book.

To my amazing wife, Emily. Thank you for not only encouraging me but rolling up your sleeves and unleashing your tremendous gifts as a writer to help me shape this book into what it ultimately is. My journey with you inspired so many of the stories woven through this book.

And to Abby, Noah, and Aaron, thank you for being inspirations to me as I see you take on the noble task of Authoring in this messy world. You do it with confidence and gusto. You are quick to pick yourselves up when you stumble, and don't let setbacks hold you down. "Resilience" doesn't fairly capture your resolve. The world needs more Authors and I'm proud that you three will contribute your own unique points of view to the bigger story that we are all a part of.

And to you, dear reader, thank you for investing your time in this book. I hope that it not only proves entertaining, but also gives you *hope and handles* as you seek to make your life and the lives around you better. After all, that's what it is all about.

Table of Contents

Preface vii

Chapter 1   The First Meeting 1

Chapter 2   Author vs. Editor 17

Chapter 3   Shifting from Author to Editor 35

Chapter 4   Clientele, Don't Clerk 55

Chapter 5   To Edit Is to Coach 73

Chapter 6   Authoring and Editing at Home 93

Chapter 7   Knowing When and How to Author as a Leader 119

Chapter 8   How to Maintain an Author vs. Editor Mindset 143

About the Author 165

Preface

A few months ago, I wrapped up a coaching call with a newly minted CEO. It was her first time in the role of CEO, and we spent our time discussing how she was struggling to let go of her prior roles and responsibilities. As we ended our time, we revisited the Author vs. Editor concept, and she observed, "It always comes down to Author versus Editor, doesn't it?" She was right. It always does.

The book in front of you holds the leadership secret to unlocking your team's potential, reclaiming your time, and maximizing your impact.

This sounds like a bold statement. But I can confidently tell you that I have been refining and teaching this concept to my coaching clients for years, and without fail, it works in almost every situation or challenge that they might be facing. Whether my client is a manager or a C-level executive, Author vs. Editor is the swiss army knife of leadership tools that can be used to maximize any vertical relationship from leading your team to influencing your manager.

Can this book help you? It can if any of the following all-too-common challenges apply to you:

- Do you feel like you are spending the majority of your time firefighting rather than fire preventing?
- Are you rolling up your sleeves and doing a lot of the work of your team?
- Are your team members routinely asking you, "What do you want me to do?"
- Do you question your team's ability to keep things on track if you weren't around?
- If you were promoted tomorrow, are you lacking a clear successor for your role?
- Does your manager regularly change your priorities and the key initiatives that she or he wants you to work on?
- Do you feel like you are constantly behind with no end in sight?
- Do you generally feel you and your team are understaffed and overworked?
- If you are a parent, do you feel overwhelmed with all of the activities and commitments of your children that require your time and involvement?

If you answered "yes" to any of the above questions, this book is for you. Throughout the pages of this book you will learn how to do the following:

Unlock your team's potential. By getting your team in the right seats, you will learn how to get them to fully take ownership, show initiative, and display critical thinking as they work to solve the problems of the organization rather than always leaning on you for the solution.

Reclaim your time. You will learn how to elevate your role, so you spend more time working "on" the business rather than "in" the business. As a result, you will find more of your time is spent on the things that only you can do given your unique role in the organization.

Maximize your impact. You will learn the art of "clienteling" with your leader so you can guide and influence their decisions in order to maximize your impact in the business. No longer will you leave meetings with your leader with a laundry list of disconnected "to do's."

And for those of you who are parents, the Author vs. Editor tool can be equally applied at home to help equip your children with the critical skills necessary to confidently Author their own paths in life.

By mastering the principles in this book, you have the power to reset your life at work and at home.

Are you ready?

Let's begin.

Chapter 1

The First Meeting

Carlos looked closely at the top right of his screen. He squinted. The clock read Tuesday, March 15, 2022, at 10:11 a.m. *It's time for new glasses*, he thought to himself. He could see his wife's look of satisfaction creep across her face when he tells her that he's finally letting go of his stubborn refusal to see the optometrist. Marisol had been after Carlos for over three years to get his eyes checked. Carlos scrolled across the screen and clicked on his calendar for the day. Like most days, his calendar was scheduled down to the minute. In addition to one-on-one meetings with members of his senior team, he had to prepare for a presentation to the board. But the meeting he was most excited about was the one that he was supposed to be having at that very moment.

Six months ago, Carlos made the difficult decision to leave his prior employer and join this new company as the CEO. It was Carlos' first time as CEO, and he was thrilled for the opportunity. Since he started the new role, Carlos had been spending all of his time not only getting a good handle on all of the strengths and weaknesses of his new company, but also trying his best to right the ship. And while there were plenty of strengths, Carlos was noticing a disturbing pattern of inefficiency and burnout with many of the leaders in the business. He was hopeful that his meeting today would shed some light on what he believed was going on.

At 10:14 a.m a slender woman in her late fifties gently opened Carlos' door. It was Carlos' executive assistant, Cynthia. She wore her graying hair in a neatly kept bun and had on an elegant pantsuit. If you didn't know better, you'd think she owned an upscale boutique. She peered through her fashionably oversized glasses to gauge Carlos' mood. She knew how much Carlos had been looking forward to this meeting, and she was curious how he was handling the absence of his guest.

Cynthia had been Carlos' executive assistant for nearly ten years and after so much time together, could read him with a glance. When Carlos accepted his new position as CEO, he convinced Cynthia to come with him.

"Would you like me to check in on him?" she asked.

Carlos picked up a worn-looking baseball off of his desk and let his fingers run over the seams. "No, I'm sure if he is running this late, there must be a very good reason," he replied.

Cynthia knew when Carlos reached for his prized baseball, it meant he was deep in thought. It was as if holding the baseball was his way of peering into a crystal ball to see the future.

She broke the silence, "Okay. I'll give him until 10:30, but then, I'm going to reach out to reschedule. As usual, you've got a full plate today, and you could use the extra time to plan and prepare for the rest of the week."

Cynthia gracefully backed out of the office and gently pulled the door closed. Carlos hardly noticed as he continued to turn the baseball in his hand, thinking about the events that led up to this meeting.

Three weeks earlier, Carlos had called an emergency senior leadership team meeting to discuss the status of the company. The entire company seemed to be stuck in the mud. Why weren't any of the key initiatives moving like they had planned? In addition, HR was hearing the same concern from all of the managers across the company. Whether the individual was a manager, a director, or a vice president, the leaders were working 65-plus hours a week. This issue seemed to be most prominently felt within the director ranks with some directors reporting 70-plus hours a week. In addition, all of the teams appeared to be in constant states of firefighting. The teams seemed to lack the competence and independence to operate independent of their manager. The result was not only an overall delay of the key initiatives for the year, but more importantly, Carlos had seen this story before. He knew how it ended, and it wasn't a pretty picture. Soon, they would start losing key leaders from sheer burnout. Their direct reports wouldn't be ready to step into those roles, and as a result there would be further delays in the initiatives. They'd have to go outside the company to look for replacements and that takes time and money. Not to mention, if too many outside hires were made, it might begin to dilute the culture Carlos had so painstakingly been building over the last five years.

That evening, Carlos shared his frustrations from the day with his wife, Marisol. Marisol reminded Carlos of the days when he too was a director and was suffering from the same symptoms that he was hearing about across the company. "Although it was nearly twenty years ago, I remember it like yesterday," Marisol said. "There were late nights at the office, weekends spent working when we hardly ever saw you, and many sleepless nights when you were trying to do it all. It seemed like you were constantly putting out fire after fire and were getting burned out in the process."

Marisol also reminded Carlos how close he had come to not only burning out but losing so much more. If it hadn't been for the conversations he had with his mentor, Carlos' story might have gone in a very different direction.

When Carlos came to the office the next day, he called a meeting with his senior team. He announced a new leadership development initiative that he wanted rolled out immediately. It was going to target all directors in the company, and it was going to entail that all members of the senior team be assigned "mentees" from this group. But unlike most formal corporate mentor programs (which Carlos had seen fail over the years), this initiative had an agenda. The members of the senior team were given a specific mandate as well as specific actions and behaviors that they were to coach these mentees to adopt. Carlos coined this program: "Operation: Author vs. Editor."

10:26 a.m. As Carlos continued to turn the baseball in his hand, he glanced down at the file in front of him titled "David Springer." Carlos opened the file, and he skimmed the first page that held all of the relevant background information. David Springer was a director in the marketing department. He was 39 years old, married with three young children, and had been with the company for ten years. He had an undergraduate degree in political science and an MBA from a well-respected school. HR had labeled David "high potential" and had David placed on the succession plan for his boss, the VP of Marketing.

Carlos flipped to the second page. It was this page that intrigued him the most. Labeled "Development Opportunities," the page not only contained highlights from David's most recent performance reviews but also the information that Carlos had asked HR to gather on each director related to their teams. It was in this particular area that Carlos' hunch had been spot on. While much of David's development areas from his performance reviews were fairly "boilerplate," there was some recent noise coming from David's team. David had lost a few key managers over the last year. From those exit interviews, the consistent theme was that while David was a "good guy," there was a firefighter culture in the department which was just unsustainable. His managers didn't feel empowered and felt like David didn't fully trust them to execute without his guidance.

If the report had stopped there, it would have been easy to simply say, "Well, this is clearly a case of a manager that is struggling with delegation and trust." However, Carlos had asked HR to also gather information from the departments that interact with David's team. Turns out, David might have some valid reasons to not let go of the reins. His team was described as "lacking ownership and initiative" by multiple internal customers. In addition, there was some concern regarding the team's ability to think strategically and execute at an acceptable level.

Just as Carlos closed the file, his office door opened. It was 10:29 a.m. Cynthia elegantly glided into the room. Behind her stood a frazzled and disheveled man. His shirt looked like it had been hastily tucked into his pants and there were several beads of sweat on his forehead. The contrast between the two individuals couldn't have been more stark. Cynthia with her calm, cool, collected, and confident presence. This young man and his look of having just barely made it out of a burning building.

Cynthia, acutely aware of David's sensitive state, said, "Carlos, I'd like to introduce you to David Springer." Carlos appreciated that Cynthia didn't rub any salt in the wound by adding, "Your 10:00 a.m appointment, by the way."

David moved forward a bit awkwardly and held out his hand. "Mr. Acosta, it is such a pleasure to meet you. I want to apologize for my tardiness. There were several last-minute issues that came up with our recent product release that required my urgent attention. In addition, we are a bit understaffed this week."

Before David could continue building his apology, Carlos sat his baseball on his desk and with the excitement of someone who was seeing a long lost relative, bounded toward David and shook his hand. "David, I am so thrilled to meet you! I have been looking forward to this meeting all week."

David was taken aback by Carlos' excitement. Of all the scenarios David had played out in his mind on how Carlos would react to his late arrival, being greeted like a returning hero was not one of them. For a split second, he almost thought Carlos was going to give him a big fatherly hug. *Maybe I won't get fired after all*, David thought to himself.

"David, please sit," Carlos said, motioning David to a small round table in the corner of the room. As David began to regain his composure and made his way to the table, Cynthia gave Carlos a knowing smile and smoothly exited the office.

Carlos took a seat across from David and continued, "David I have been going over your file. You have accomplished a great deal during your time here. Your manager has nothing but glowing things to say about you and, in full transparency, we have big plans for you here. Let me ask you a question. When this meeting was scheduled, was there anything you wanted to make sure we discussed? Or more specifically, is there anything I can help you with?"

David thought for a moment. He wasn't sure how to answer the question. Not only was David unsure of the purpose of the meeting, but frankly, he had not given it much thought. He just knew it was part of a corporate mentoring program that had recently been rolled out. *Something about Operation Auditor*, David thought. When the matches were made between directors and the executives, David had unfortunately gotten the CEO as his match. If his life wasn't stressful enough, now he had to regularly meet with the CEO as part of this program. David felt like he was about to go on an extended six-month interview, and if this first meeting was any indication of how this was going to go for him, he was not looking forward to it.

"Mr. Acosta, I am truly grateful for your time. I don't have a particular agenda for our time together. I just thought it might be a good opportunity to learn from you and take any guidance or direction you might like to provide me." David, reached down into his leather bag, he pulled out a notebook, opened it and clicked his pen into action. He paused as if he was waiting for wisdom or instructions to spew forth from Carlos.

Carlos responded, "David, I figured that might be the case. We were not very clear on the purpose of these meetings by design. We wanted to see how our leaders approached the opening conversation. Consider it a simple diagnostic."

David's wheels were turning. *That first question was a test? So, I'm 30 minutes late to my first meeting with the CEO and I fail the first test he gives me. Yep, I'm going to get fired.* David's shoulders noticeably slumped.

Carlos noticed David's change in demeanor and continued, "David, this is not meant to be some sort of test. As I mentioned, consider it a diagnostic. And like any diagnostic, I'm just trying to identify the best way I can be of service to you. To that end, I have a few more of those types of questions for you today, so I can get a better sense of what is working for you and what might be some areas for us to explore together." Carlos pulled out a notepad of his own and flipped to a blank page. "In a given week, how many hours do you think you are working? Remember, this is a diagnostic question. There are no 'right' or 'wrong' answers. Just do your very best to be honest with me." Carlos paused and waited for David's response.

David thought about it. It wasn't unusual for him to work 12-hour days. In addition, he usually spent most of Sunday afternoon working. Ally, his wife, had been trying to get him to cut back, but it seemed like just when he would start to put in place better boundaries, there would be another fire to deal with.

"I guess if I was 100% honest, it is probably close to 70 hours a week," David hesitantly replied. Carlos jotted a few things down on his notepad. "Thanks David. Exactly what I'm looking for. Here's my next question. Think back to your last vacation. How much did you work while you were on vacation?" Carlos paused and looked at David for his response.

David distinctly remembered the last vacation they took as a family because of the fight that he and Ally had gotten into. They had taken the kids to Disney World for the first time last year. What was supposed to have been a fun family vacation full of laughter, rides, and new experiences together, ended up with David staying in the hotel room for two of the days to, as he put it, "Put out some fires." And when he was at the parks with his family, he was on his cell phone taking work calls while they waited in line for the rides. Needless to say, Ally was not happy.

"My last vacation was a particularly bad example of this," responded David. "I would say I worked about 50% of the time."

Carlos nodded his head in understanding and began jotting a few more notes down on his notepad. "David, I want to shift our conversation a bit to specifically talking about your team. How often do you hear from your direct reports the phrase, 'What do you want me to do?'"

David didn't have to hesitate on this. He pulled out his phone and opened an email from one of his direct reports earlier that morning. "I think it would be easier to give you an example. This is an e-mail that I received at approximately 9:45 a.m this morning. It is from one of my direct reports." David began to read the email aloud:

David,

The product launch intended for this afternoon has hit a significant snag. We have not yet received the necessary approval from legal and the e-commerce team has yet to deliver their communication plan to us as promised. We have been waiting patiently, but still no word from either group. Please advise on how you would like us to proceed.

Meghan Sterbo
Sr. Manager
Marketing and Product Development

After David read the email to Carlos, he continued, "I get emails like this all day long, every day. It is incredibly frustrating that I have to jump into the middle of every project in order to keep things on schedule."

Carlos could tell that David was exacerbated. He could also tell that David was starting to lower his guard. *Good,* Carlos thought to himself. *He's going to need to trust me if I am going to be able to help him.* Carlos jotted a few more notes down, and then lifted his head once more to David. "David, thanks for all of your honesty and candor. I have two last questions for you today. Here is the first one: If I promoted you tomorrow, who would you recommend as your replacement?"

Unlike Carlos' last question, David did not have a quick response. He stared out Carlos' office window as he mentally evaluated each of his direct reports. One by one, David had reasonable and valid concerns that took each direct report out of the running for his job. From a lack of initiative to difficulty in prioritizing, not one of his direct reports were ready for the next step. After a few moments in deep thought, David responded to Carlos' question. "While I am quite proud of my team and their accomplishments, I can honestly say that none of my direct reports are ready for the next step at this time."

Carlos jotted a few more notes on his pad and then continued, "Okay David. Last question. If I promoted you tomorrow and gave you more responsibility and a significant bump in pay, what would your wife say?"

David froze. This question seemed to touch on something very sensitive. As David continued to process the question, Carlos studied the features on David's face very closely. It was as if the color was being drained as David became paler and paler. Carlos decided to let the silence and discomfort play out. He sat patiently and waited. Finally, David broke the silence.

"Mr. Acosta, if you offered me a promotion tomorrow, I would have two choices in front of me. First, I could take the promotion and face a high probability of my wife divorcing me. Or second, I could turn down the offer knowing I would likely be committing career suicide if I continued to stay here. Opportunities like that don't come along very often, and I would be labeled as either lacking confidence or lacking ambition, neither of which would be seen as good executive material. I would need to get my resume together and begin looking for another job." David stopped talking and slumped in his chair. He looked utterly and completely defeated. What if this meeting had been about offering David the next role? If so, he just blew it.

After hanging his head for a few seconds, David glanced up at Carlos expecting to see a look of disappointment. Instead, what he saw was an expression on Carlos' face that was full of understanding. Carlos had a wide grin on his face. Carlos closed his notepad and put his pen down. He took off his glasses and rested them on top of the notepad.

With a smirk as if he had just solved a complicated mystery, Carlos spoke. "David, first, thank you for entertaining me and my questions. Your responses were exactly as I had hoped: honest, transparent, vulnerable, and real. I was hoping to learn about some of the pain points that you face on a day-to-day basis as a leader, and you helped me to see that quite well. In addition, your answers were very much what I was expecting to hear. I'd like to tell you about one of the most challenging times in my life when I was a director just like you, but before I share that with you, from now on, please call me Carlos."

The Seat Dilemma

Several years ago, I took my kids on a mini summer vacation. Usually, our trips consisted of my wife and my three kiddos and myself, but this trip was different. My wife had a separate trip planned so it was just the four of us. We were excited for the trip, and the kiddos had an active hand in planning the details. I had banked a lot of airline miles up to that point in the year, so I thought, *Why not use my miles for the kids' tickets*? So that's what I did. Now, like many frequent travelers, I had gotten sucked into the "airline status" game. I wanted to collect as many airline points as possible for myself during the year, so I could not only maintain my current status with the airline, but maybe, just maybe, I would get to the envied next level. So, what did I do? I used points for the kids' tickets and purchased my own tickets with my airline credit card. A great plan, right? Yes, except when we got to the gate to board the plane, the ticket agents excitedly greeted me by saying, "Mr. Smith, we are pleased to let you know that you have been upgraded to seat 1B in First Class."

Now, on most any day, that would be fine. But on this particular occasion, moving to First Class would have meant that my three minor children would be sitting in coach by themselves. Abby, Noah, and Aaron have always been fiercely independent, so they had no issue with the new arrangement. In fact, they were happy for me. "Dad, you should totally sit in First Class," prompted Abby. "How cool." And while I appreciated her enthusiasm, it didn't change the fact that I was sitting in the wrong seat for this flight and that just wasn't going to do. I needed to fix this seat problem ASAP.

The seat dilemma is a real dilemma for almost every leader that I encounter. They were "assigned" one seat (Ex: We want you to oversee and guide the performance of this function/team), and yet, when "the flight is about to take off," they feel it necessary to switch seats to another part of the plane. They find themselves "doing" the work of their teams when they should be "leading" the work. Put another way, they find themselves "in" the business and not working "on" the business. Can you relate? Most likely, you can.

There are a variety of reasons you, as a leader, may find yourself sitting in the seat where you are dictating and orchestrating the details of the work rather than the seat where you are guiding, coaching, and leading the work. Consider whether the following sound all too familiar to you:

- There is constant pressure to get too much done without enough time.
- Everything is urgent all of the time. Everything is covered in "hot sauce."
- You aren't in a culture that tolerates even the smallest mistake or misstep.

- You find yourself reluctant to let go of the "how" of the work for fear that your team will "cook the recipe" all wrong.
- The hero trap. You are a great hero. There is an emotional/ego payoff in being able to swoop in and solve problems on a regular basis for your team and they are quick to call on you.
- You don't want to put too much strain on your team by asking too much of them.

When we sit in the wrong seat for extended periods of time, there are some significant symptoms that emerge. If not addressed, these symptoms lead to frustration, turnover, burnout, low team performance, and an inability to operate strategically. More simply put, we will hit a career brick wall. The wall will be so insurmountable that there will be no way to simply work longer hours to get through it. Harder work won't solve the problem.

Signs You Are Spending Too Much Time in the Wrong Seat

How can you tell if you are suffering from sitting in the wrong seat? Take the following quiz to see if you are suffering from a "seat problem":

1. Consider how many hours a week you are working. The chart below may help you identify the degree to which this is a likely problem for you (*Note:* the following hours are based on the work hours of a typical "director" role in most organizations):

Hours Worked in a Typical Week	Diagnosis
40–50 hours	You are likely balancing your responsibilities well and have a solid handle on what "seat" you need to be sitting in in any given situation (Congratulations! You are in the top 5%).
50–65 hours	There is a strong probability that you are sitting in the wrong seat more often than you should.
65–75 hours	It is highly likely that you are sitting in the wrong seat in the majority of your interactions with your direct reports and your manager.
75+ hours	It is almost certain that you are sitting in the wrong seat in most situations. While this could be a byproduct of understaffing, it is also likely you are putting yourself in the wrong seat when given the option. This is an unsustainable position for most.

2. **Your team is not self-sufficient without you.** If you were promoted, exited the company, or were hit by a bus, your team would not be able to step up to the call. ***Yes or No***
3. **You feel like your actual job title should change to "firefighter."** As you think about the amount of time you spend each and every week, the strong majority of your time (over 90%) is dedicated to firefighting with very little time spent on planning and fire-preventing. ***Yes or No***
4. **You feel like you never have time to actually do the job you are paid and hired to do.** With all of the fires, where's the time to do the strategic stuff? ***Yes or No***
5. **When you go to meetings with your manager, you let her/him drive the agenda.** You wait for them to tell you what you should do before you take action. ***Yes or No***
6. **It feels like your manager either makes everything a priority or is changing priorities too frequently.** You can never seem to keep up with what is on her or his mind. ***Yes or No***
7. **Your partner (or family/friends, if more applicable) regularly complains to you about how much you work during weekends, vacations, and other "non-work" hours.** You can distinctly remember missing an important "personal event" over the last year that required damage control. ***Yes or No***

If you answered "Yes" to the majority of the questions above, <u>this book is for you</u>.

Let me be clear. Despite what you may have been led to believe, your issue is not time management. Nor is your issue delegation or trust. You suffer from a "seat" problem.

This book is about helping leaders like you identify the right seat to sit in at the right time in order to get you from working "in" the business to "on" the business. When we sit in the right seat, we not only elevate our performance, but it is the path to building high-performing teams around us. It is the path to truly leading.

This book holds the leadership secret that very few leaders know and practice today. By mastering this secret, you will be able to elevate your leadership to levels you've never experienced, put your team on the path to high-performance, regain your work/life balance and forge your path to unlimited leadership opportunities.

Going back to my seat dilemma, you may be wondering, what did I do when my seat was reassigned? Without giving it a second thought, I sat down next to my kiddos in my original seat, 32B. When the new occupant of 32B approached and saw me sitting in his place, he calmly said, "I think you might be sitting in my seat." I responded, "Yes, I know. How about a trade?" I handed him my newly printed ticket for 1B. Without hesitation, he took the ticket and replied "deal."

We don't have to blindly accept the seat "assigned" to us. We have the power to intentionally *choose* the seat that is the right one for us and for those around us. It just takes a little courage, clarity, and faith.

CHAPTER 2

Author vs. Editor

20 years earlier...

It was a rainy Spring evening in 2002. Carlos was trying to navigate his way home through a sudden downpour. The windshield wipers on Carlos' car worked angrily. The rain was coming down harder now. Carlos gripped the steering wheel a little more tightly. He squinted. To a casual observer, Carlos' squint would have appeared to be in reaction to the treacherous weather conditions. Afterall, visibility on the roads was practically nonexistent at this point. But the reality was that Carlos was having a hard time keeping his eyes open. He was exhausted. It was 8:45 p.m. on a Friday and Carlos was just now heading home from work.

As he thought back to the week, he was sure he had logged at last 75 hours in the office. It seems like these types of weeks had become Carlos' normal routine since he was promoted to director. Carlos had told himself that once he settled into the role, things would start to get a little more "normal." The problem is that his promotion occurred over a year ago. That excuse just wasn't going to work anymore. When his boss announced Carlos' promotion, Carlos remembers excitedly telling his wife. Finally, he had arrived, and all his hard work had paid off. Carlos remembers the glow of pride he saw on Marisol's face when he gave her the news. That look alone made it all worth it. They went out that night and celebrated at the most popular steakhouse in town, Cuts, and even hired a babysitter to watch the kids.

Carlos and Marisol hadn't been out to dinner as a couple since. Carlos has missed birthdays, anniversaries, baseball games, dance recitals, and countless other important life events. Perhaps this was more top of mind for Carlos because he was supposed to have been home over two hours ago to celebrate his mother's birthday. His parents were coming over and Marisol had a special dinner planned that included making her famous rum cake. Carlos had repeatedly promised that he would be home by 6:30 p.m. and not a minute later. When Carlos called home to let Marisol know that he was going to be late, she didn't say a word. The silence was worse than anything she could have said at that moment. He could tell that she had reached her tipping point. Things were going to have to change if Carlos wanted to keep his marriage intact.

Carlos' thoughts moved back to the present. The rain was letting up ever so slightly. Suddenly, Carlos realized that he didn't know where he was. The rain combined with his exhaustion had resulted in Carlos missing a turn on his way home. He was officially lost. He found his way to an empty bank parking lot and pulled into a space. He noticed that he was still gripping the steering wheel tightly. His knuckles were white. *How symbolic*, he thought to himself.

His lack of progress over this past year wasn't for a lack of trying. And yet, despite Carlos' efforts, he found himself in the same place he where he started a year ago. His team hasn't really developed the way he had hoped, and if anything is going to get done, he has to be actively involved. It honestly feels like he is rolling up his sleeves and doing the work of his direct reports as well as his own. And while he has enjoyed being shoulder-to-shoulder with his team, if he was honest with himself, he rarely has time in a given week to do his actual job.

And he wasn't doing his job at home either. He wasn't being the husband that he wanted to be. Marisol's silence on the call earlier today was a reminder of that. And he wasn't being the dad that he wanted to be. He had hoped to coach baseball for his youngest this Fall, but he knew he couldn't commit to the practice and game schedule given the state of things at work. Something had to give.

The rain finally relented. At that moment, the answer came to Carlos. He reached into his bag from work and found his address book. He flipped pages until he got to his destination. His finger moved to the number he was looking for. He dug into his bag and found his cell phone. He was lucky that he had just enough cell coverage to place the call. He dialed the number and waited. After a few rings, a voice answered. "Hello?"

"Professor Cooper, this is Carlos Acosta, one of your former MBA students from a few years ago."

Professor Marilyn Cooper was famous not only for her work in the classroom, but she also had a long list of accomplished leaders that called her "mentor." Carlos knew she would have a solution to his dilemma.

"Oh Carlos, of course I remember you," Professor Cooper responded. "It is such a pleasure to hear from you," she responded. "How can I be of assistance?"

Carlos spent the next fifteen minutes catching Marilyn Cooper up on his recent career accomplishments, and more importantly, the challenges he had been dealing with over the last year. Marilyn patiently listened only to interrupt on occasion to ask a few clarifying questions. Finally, Marilyn responded.

"Carlos, you have an Author versus Editor problem."

"A what problem?" asked Carlos.

Marilyn continued, "You have an Author versus Editor problem. It is a 'seat' problem, you see." She paused briefly, then continued, "In order for you to be successful as a leader, you have to know what seat to sit in given the situation and context. Based on what you have described to me, it sounds like you have been sitting in the wrong seat way too often. This often results in doing work that you shouldn't be doing, long hours at work, an underdeveloped team, and no real time to do your actual job."

Carlos paused for a minute to reflect on how happy he was that he called Marilyn. She nailed it. "That is exactly what I'm dealing with. So, is there a solution? Because I don't think I can continue this way for much longer." Carlos swallowed hard and held his breath as he waited for her response. There needs to be a solution for this, or he was going to have to consider other more desperate measures.

"Carlos, of course there is a solution," Marilyn responded cheerfully. "I want you to meet me at FOOD 643 tomorrow for lunch," she continued. FOOD 643 was one of the hottest restaurants in town.

"Professor Cooper, I really appreciate your help, and I don't mean to sound ungrateful, but FOOD 643 is typically booked months in advance. I'm not sure we would be able to get in. Maybe we should meet at someplace a little less popular," Carlos said.

Marilyn calmly replied, "Carlos, there is nothing to worry about. I know the owner quite well. In fact, he is the reason why I want us to meet there. Can you meet me there at 11:45 a.m. tomorrow? Oh, and Carlos, since you are no longer my student, please call me Marilyn."

FOOD 643 occupied the top floor of a high rise downtown. There was a separate elevator that went to the restaurant. A small stand and two staff members guarded the exclusive elevator. It was understood by any casual observer that if you didn't have a reservation, you weren't getting on that elevator. At precisely 11:45 a.m., Carlos hesitantly approached the stand.

"How can we help you today?" asked one of the staff members.

"I'm meeting Professor Marilyn Cooper today for an 11:45 a.m. reservation," Carlos cautiously replied.

Without missing a beat, the other staff member responded, "Yes. You must be Carlos Acosta. We have been expecting you. Dr. Cooper is waiting for you upstairs. We will let them know that you are on your way. Please enter the elevator and there will be a staff member to greet you when you arrive."

As Carlos was led to his table, he saw Marilyn already seated. She looked just as he remembered her. She had short silver hair that was cropped elegantly. She glanced up from the menu and when she saw Carlos approaching, she greeted him. "Carlos, it is so good to see you. I'm thrilled that you were able to make it. Given your Author-Editor problem, I was half expecting to hear from the staff that you were unable to make it."

If it had been anyone else, Carlos might have been offended by the comment, but Marilyn said it with a look of true care and compassion in her eyes. Carlos sat down. After a few minutes of small talk, he brought the conversation back to something that had been on his mind since last night. "Marilyn, you keep mentioning this Author and Editor thing. I don't think I fully understand what you are talking about. Can you elaborate a bit more?"

Marilyn smiled. "Of course. Here is how the concept works. In any dynamic between a manager and a direct report, someone always has to sit in the Author seat, and someone has to sit in the Editor seat. It is critical to understand that both of those seats have to be filled. Now, let's talk about those seats." Marilyn forged ahead with her explanation:

> *"The Author seat is about doing the work. When we sit in the Author seat we take ownership, show initiative, and display critical thinking. We proactively problem-solve and Author solutions."*

She added, "The individuals that naturally take to 'Authorship' are often the ones that get recognized as high potentials in any organization."

Marilyn paused and took a drink of water. "Now, let's talk about the Editor seat. The Editor does not do the work. The Editor 'Edits' the work. They set overall expectations for what they are looking for, and when the Author presents their work to the Editor, the Editor's job is to make the work better." She paused a moment to rephrase and really emphasize the Editor's role:

> *"In short, the Editor seat is a coaching seat. It is all about helping to elevate not only the quality of the work of the Author but also the level of critical thinking displayed by the Author."*

At some point during her dialogue, Carlos had pulled out a notebook and began frantically taking notes. He made sure to capture this last point.

Marilyn continued, "When leaders sit in the Editor seat, they are working to elevate the performance of their direct reports. When done effectively, it allows that leader to not only build a high performing team under him or her, but also to shift their time so they are working 'on' the business instead of 'in' the business. This is arguably the journey to becoming a truly effective leader."

Marilyn paused, took another drink of water, and looked over at Carlos.

"I think I understand the concept," replied Carlos. "I pride myself on taking ownership, showing initiative and being a problem solver. That is probably why I was promoted." Marilyn nodded in agreement. Carlos continued, "And now in my current role, I'm still doing that. I'm trying to 'Author' myself and my team into a better place." Marilyn gave another nod of approval. "So, it sounds like what I need to do is find someone or maybe a training program, that I can send my team to so they can get proper 'Editing.'"

Carlos waited for another nod from Marilyn, but instead she scrunched her face as if she had just tasted something sour. Before Carlos could continue, she interjected "Carlos, you can't outsource the Editor role. That is *your* job. You need to learn to move from doing the work to helping your team to do the work. This will free you up so you have more time to not only do more strategic work, working 'on' the business, but you might also find you have more time to spend with your family."

Carlos was confused. He always prided himself on his work ethic. He was constantly recognized by his boss and other leaders in the company for his ability to jump in and solve problems. He had a reputation of not quitting until the job was done right. It sounded like what Marilyn was asking him to do was to abandon all that made him the rising star that he had become in the company.

"I just don't know if I can completely let go like that. My boss relies on me to make sure everything gets done on time and at the highest quality. If I'm not actively involved, I just don't know if those expectations will be met." Just as Carlos finished his response, a tall man wearing a crisp white chef uniform approached the table.

"Simon, it is so good to see you," Marilyn said as she stood up to greet the chef. "Carlos, this is Simon Black. He is the owner of FOOD 643 as well as several other amazing restaurants around town."

"Marilyn, you are too kind," responded Simon. Carlos noticed that Simon had an Australian accent. He had short, neatly trimmed brown hair with just a few hints of silver and was clean shaven. If Carlos was to guess, he would put Simon not a day over 40, just a few years older than himself.

Simon reached his hand out to Carlos. "And you must be Carlos. I am so thrilled to meet you. When Marilyn called me last night and explained your situation, I knew we needed to meet. In addition to also being a former student of Marilyn, I too had an Author versus Editor problem that nearly broke me."

After a few more minutes of conversation, Carlos learned that after working in some of the top restaurants in Sydney, Simon moved to the United States and worked in several world-renowned restaurants in New York City before opening his own restaurant about eight years ago. His restaurant opened to rave reviews. But after just three years of running the restaurant, Simon was burned out. He was in the restaurant seven days a week. He was not only handling all of the business elements of the restaurant, but also, he was personally cooking every meal coming out of the kitchen. He had a staff, but he didn't trust them with anything "critical." The only way Simon could maintain the level of quality that he expected in every dish was to get involved in every detail.

One day, he came home from work and found a note on the kitchen counter from his wife. She had decided to take the kids and go back to Australia for a few months to visit with family and friends. She was lonely. That was Simon's wake up call. He knew something had to change.

Despite the incredible success of his restaurant, Simon made the difficult decision to close the restaurant and reset. He enrolled in an Executive MBA program in hopes of learning better ways to manage and lead. It was during his first semester that he took Professor Cooper's class on leadership and organizational management. As Simon put it, "It opened my eyes wider than they had ever been opened."

After Marilyn's course, Simon reached out to several of his former staff and began planning a relaunch of the restaurant, but this time Simon was going to be sitting in the right seat at the right time. Six months later Simon opened Cuts steakhouse and hasn't looked back. FOOD 643 is Simon's fourth restaurant and he has plans to open several more over the next few years.

"Carlos, I want to show you something. Come with me to the kitchen, and I think you'll get a better understanding of the changes that I made," said Simon.

When they entered the kitchen, Carlos was overwhelmed with all of the activity. Chefs were busily working at each station with a level of precision and focus that Carlos admired. As dishes were prepared, they went to a station where they awaited a server, but before they left the kitchen, another chef had the job of reviewing each dish for quality. After approving a few dishes for delivery, Carlos noticed the

Editor chef pick up one of the dishes and walk it back to its originating station. He calmly placed it in front of the chef that prepared it, and after a brief discussion and some head nodding from the chef that Authored the dish, the Editor walked away as the Author chef began reworking the meal.

Simon leaned over to Carlos and whispered, "Just five years ago, I would have been doing all of this myself. The only thing I relied on my staff for was simple tasks like chopping, cutting, basic cooking, and plating. Look at what I missed out on. In fact, half of the recipes on the menu aren't even mine. These amazing people came up with those dishes on their own. I just had to give them the opportunity to take ownership, show initiative, and display critical thinking. Once I did that, amazing things began to happen."

Carlos and Simon walked back to the table where Marilyn was peering through her reading glasses as she studied the menu. Carlos thanked Simon for his time and sat down across from Marilyn as Simon headed back to the kitchen. Carlos couldn't help but notice the confidence and, more importantly, measured pace at which Simon walked. *He had things in control*, Carlos thought.

"Well, what did you learn?" Marilyn inquired. Carlos shared his many observations and insights from the kitchen tour. After some more reassuring nods, Marilyn asked "So, what are you going to do?" Carlos took a deep breath. He was surprised that even though the kitchen experience was inspiring and empowering, he was feeling anxious about what he had to do next. He laid out his plan to Marilyn. Carlos' plan was received with more head nodding from Marilyn, signaling her approval.

"When do you intend to put your plan in place?" she challenged.

"I plan on starting as soon as I get back to the office this afternoon," Carlos responded confidently.

"Well then, let's enjoy one of Simon and his team's amazing creations as a celebration of starting a new chapter," responded Marilyn.

The meal was delicious.

The Concept

The Author vs. Editor concept is simple yet powerful. In short, in any interaction between a manager and a direct report, someone has to sit in the Author seat, and someone has to sit in the Editor seat. The key is to know which seat to sit in at the proper time. Ideally, the manager should be spending the majority of her or his time (approximately 80%) sitting in the Editor seat when working with her or his direct reports, and should only sit in the Author seat in particular circumstances (approximately 20%).

Let's test this idea with your own experiences. Take a moment to think about your all-time favorite direct reports. My hunch is that when there was a problem or issue, they would likely come to you saying something akin to, "There is a problem. Here is what I think we should do about it. I would love to get your thoughts." They come with what I call an Authored solution for you to Edit.

Now, think about your less-than-best direct reports. In that same situation, they would likely come to you very differently. They would say something like, "There is a problem. What do you want me to do about it?" They would expect *you* to Author a solution, allowing *them* to sit in the Editor seat (remember, both seats have to be filled). Then if things don't go as planned, they can always say, "It's not my fault. I just did what I was told to do."

In order to better understand the concept and its importance, let's take a deeper dive into each of the "seats."

The Editor Seat

When we sit in the Editor Seat, there are a few important roles that we play. First and foremost, as it would be with any traditional Editor, our job is to help the Author make her or his work product a *"New York Times* bestseller." Using this analogy, as the Editor we don't write the book for the Author. We don't say, "I know what a *New York Times* bestseller looks like. In fact, I've written several of my own. I'll just write it for you and then you can put your name on it."

That would be ridiculous. And yet, how often have we done that very thing with our direct reports? We do their work for them because, after all, not only have we done it before, but we were probably pretty good at it. In fact, it was likely our skill in those roles that resulted in us getting promoted into the leadership role we're currently in.

Rather than doing the work for our direct reports, when we sit in the Editor seat, we are playing the role of coach.

As the Editor, our goal is to elevate our direct reports' critical thinking and the quality of their work product.

Consider the following important traits and activities of the Editor:

- **The Editor Sets Expectations.** The Editor sets of the Author. They clearly define what the end state like, but do not dictate the path to get there.

Consider the concept of "Commander's Intent" that is utilized in the United States Military. When there is a new mission or objective, the commanding officer calls a meeting with his or her direct reports and issues the "why" of the mission, the "what" of the mission and the "when" of the mission. They stay away from the "how" of the mission because there are too many variables on the battlefield. In addition, there is an understanding that every soldier needs to be able to step up and lead if the situation arises. They cannot be effective if they are always waiting for someone to give them an order. They must be able to step back, assess the situation at hand, and make an informed decision as to how to move forward.

The Editor's critical role is to share his or her "Commander's Intent" for the team while allowing the team to define the "how."

- **The Editor Coaches.** In order to improve their direct reports' critical thinking, their approach to problem solving, and their overall work product, the Editor must be willing to be a coach.

In order for the Editor to be effective in this role, several things must happen. First and foremost, the Editor must require that the Author bring something for her or him to react to. As a manager, if you aren't requiring your direct report to bring anything to a meeting for you to react to (Edit), you will find yourself Authoring or co-Authoring work rather than truly helping them improve their ability to Author independent of you.

Second, these meetings have to be intentionally scheduled and planned. For example, if there is a big presentation to leadership in two weeks, you might say to your direct report something like, "Our presentation is in two weeks. On Friday, I want to review the first draft of the presentation. Come to the meeting with a first draft prepared so we can review, discuss, and Edit."

It sounds quite simple, but if you are like most managers, you are meeting with your direct reports regularly to attend to fires and to deal with emerging issues, but there isn't a clear agenda, and we rarely require that our direct reports bring us something for us to react to. As a result, we are doing our team members a disservice. We never give them the time, attention and coaching to help them improve.

- **The Editor Encourages the Author's Agency.** The Editor does not solve the problem for the direct report. Rather, they require their direct report to provide a point of view. They require that the direct report dictate the how and take ownership of the situation.

Consider this example. I recently had a client with an underperforming employee. In essence, my client's direct report was struggling with truly taking ownership and responsibility for his tasks, resulting in lackluster performance. As my client put it, "He seems to lack passion and strategic thinking." In addition, whenever something didn't go as planned, there was always an excuse and someone or something to blame. In short, this employee was reluctant to Author.

My client had reached the point where he was ready to put this employee on a performance improvement plan. As you may be familiar, in these cases a manager would sit an employee down, discuss the issue with her or him, and then present the employee with a plan to improve their performance. If the employee is unsuccessful in the allotted time provided (typically between 30–90 days), they would be "invited to leave." Here's the fundamental problem with this traditional approach. The manager is Authoring the plan for the employee.

If we truly want to promote ownership, which is critical with performance improvement, we need to require that the individual draft the plan. We shouldn't be writing it for her or him. When we require others to Author the plan, it promotes ownership and increases the probability of success. My client took this approach and immediately started to see a positive change with his direct report.

Sitting in the Editor seat with our team is the path to creating a high-performing team that can function independent of us. This allows us to move from working "in" the business to "on" the business. Now, let's consider the Author seat.

The Author Seat

When our team members (or us, for that matter) sit in the Author seat, they are taking ownership, showing initiative, and displaying critical thinking. Authors solve problems. Authors put out fires. Authors are "all in" and display high levels of commitment and a desire to take on responsibility. A team full of properly trained Authors is critical if we, as leaders, want to go from working "in" the business to "on" the business.

Consider the following important traits of the Author:

- **The Author Takes Ownership.** The Author has a sense of pride and ownership in their work product. When they pick something up, they carry it all the way to the end. But more importantly, they don't need to be told to take ownership. They seek it out. They are not afraid of responsibility. In fact, they crave it. They like being held accountable and responsible for results because of the challenge it presents.

- **The Author Shows Initiative.** The Author does not require an invitation for change. When they see a need, they take action. They don't wait to be told what to do. They are the first to raise their hand and volunteer to take on an assignment or project. They proactively set up meetings with their manager, their colleagues, and their customers. They are on their toes and not on their heels. They move with a sense of urgency.

- **The Author Displays Critical Thinking.** The Author spends time assessing the situation around them. They bring a point of view to any conversation. They can quickly analyze any situation or problem. An Author can then turn that analysis into recommendations, strategy, and a path forward. They trust their instincts and have confidence in their ability to solve any problem that might come their way.

When you combine ownership, initiative, and critical thinking, you have an individual that sees a problem and quickly moves into action. And with the guidance of an Editor, they will move with precision and accuracy toward the goals and outcomes the organization has identified as most important.

But therein lies the rub. Regardless of our level in an organization, when we Author well, we get recognized as High Potentials and we get promoted. And once promoted, we can have a hard time handing over the Author reins. We have a tendency to step in and take ownership, show initiative, and display critical thinking rather than shifting to the Editor seat we've been promoted to with our team.

One final point to note: Overall, we should be spending the majority of our time Editing down and Authoring up. Just as our team should be Authoring solutions for us to Edit, we should be Authoring solutions, recommendations, and a point of view to our manager for her or him to Edit.

When everyone in the system Authors up and Edits down, the organization is highly efficient and effective.

Leaders can get a tremendous amount of work done in a nice neat 40 hours. However, when the flow is reversed and we Author down to our team, doing their work for them or micromanaging the details, they're allowed to sit in the Editor seat. When our team is stuck in the Editor seat and we Author for them, they're not taking ownership, not showing initiative, and not displaying critical thinking, and it causes significant issues. This "reversed flow" can be even more challenging if our leader is Authoring down to us insisting on being involved in every decision and not empowering us. The result is that we can find ourselves burning the candle at both ends, working 75-plus hours a week.

Reflection Questions for You from Chapter 2

- Rate yourself: How much time do you spend sitting in the Editor Seat with your team? How often do you Author your team's work for them?
- Have you clearly communicated your "Commander's Intent" to your team, so they clearly know your expectations?
- When did you do this? In what way did you communicate it? Email / Group Meeting / One-on-One, etc.
- Do you require that your direct reports bring Authored items to your meetings for you to Edit?
- How do you encourage "Ownership, Initiative, and Critical Thinking" from your team?
- Where would you like to see your Team improve in this area?
- How do you display "Ownership, Initiative, and Critical Thinking" with your manager?
- How would you like to improve in this area?

CHAPTER 3

Shifting from Author to Editor

CARLOS BARELY MADE it back from the restaurant in time for his first afternoon meeting. As he plopped down in his chair, he grabbed a tissue and mopped the sweat from his brow. His mind was bouncing back and forth between preparing for the meeting he was about to have and his eye-opening experience at the restaurant. Carlos felt exhilarated, still on a high from the conversation at lunch. Everything he experienced, from the dynamic kitchen to Simon's story, and, of course, Marilyn's wise words, were playing out in his head. Carlos felt a combination of excitement and uneasiness as he thought about putting what he heard into action. Could he pull this off? How would his team react to his new approach?

Unfortunately, he wasn't going to have much time to think about it. Carlos had a full calendar of one-on-one meetings the entire afternoon with members of his team. He took a deep breath and thought to himself, *It's now or never.*

Sandra was Carlos' 1:00 p.m. meeting. Sandra had been a member of Carlos' team for nearly three years. When Carlos was promoted, he lobbied to have Sandra elevated to a Sr. Manager so she could continue to be a direct report. Sandra's dedication and hard work were unmatched. She was by far the highest performer on his team. That said, he always felt like he took the lead in their conversations. After his conversation with Simon and Marilyn, he realized that was going to have to change.

A minute before the hour, Sandra lightly tapped on Carlos' door. After Carlos invited her in, they moved to a small table with two chairs in the corner of Carlos' office. Carlos' office wasn't very large so Carlos' request for an additional table and chairs was met with some raised eyebrows from maintenance. That didn't dissuade the persistent Carlos. He never liked the dynamic of looking across his desk at a direct report. It didn't feel like they were on the same team. He wanted a table so he could have more open conversations and the feeling that he was rolling up his sleeves alongside whoever he was meeting.

After Sandra was settled in her seat, Carlos opened the conversation, "What would you like to discuss today?"

Sandra's calm demeanor noticeably shifted. She wrung her hands for a moment uncertain of what to do, then quickly regained her composure. "Well, I thought we'd discuss whatever you had in mind for this meeting."

This might be a bit more challenging than I had thought, noted Carlos. Carlos started, "Sandra, you and I have worked together for many years. I think you know how much I value and appreciate you. All that said, I have to apologize to you. In an effort to support you and provide clear guidance, I have inadvertently held you back from inserting your unique point of view. I'd like to change that. Starting today, when we have meetings, I want you to bring your point of view to each and every discussion. This can be related to your team, our department, or the business. I don't want to do anything to hold you back from feeling a sense of ownership, the ability to take initiative, and offering your unique perspective on the things we are dealing with on a day-to-day basis." Carlos paused and waited for Sandra's reaction.

Sandra took a moment to process what she'd heard. After reflecting, she confidently responded, "I appreciate your belief in me, Carols, and I look forward to offering some more specific recommendations and perspectives on how we can improve things around here."

That was the start to one of the best one-on-one meetings Carlos had had with his direct reports in many months. Sandra offered ideas, opinions, and perspectives that he'd never considered. They didn't always agree, but the discussion made Carlos realize he didn't have to carry the burden of being the only critical thinker and problem-solver on the team; Sandra was more than capable to play that role as well.

Carlos had three more similar conversations that afternoon with his team members. All of the conversations, based on Carlos' initial estimates, went well. While not all team members jumped feet first into dialogue with Carlos, all of his direct reports verbally agreed to Carlos' new approach to meetings. He was feeling incredibly optimistic.

A week later, Carlos braced himself for his follow-up conversations. He realized these would be the true test to determine the effectiveness of his new approach. Just as he did the prior week, he began with his one-on-one conversation with Sandra. In typical fashion, at one minute before the hour, Sandra tapped lightly on Carlos' office. And as usual, Carlos ushered Sandra into the office and directed her to the small table in the corner.

However, that was where "as usual" came to an end. Unlike prior meetings, Sandra reached for her bag and pulled out a thin manilla folder. She opened the folder and took out two copies of the enclosed document, smoothly slid one copy across the table to Carlos and kept the other copy neatly in front of her. "I have prepared an overview of what I would like to discuss today," she opened.

Carlos glanced at the document and couldn't contain his enthusiasm. Sandra had done a masterful job of not only outlining the current problems and issues facing her team, but also had evaluated possible scenarios and skillfully identified practical recommendations.

Carlos glanced up and said to Sandra, "This is quite impressive. Tell me more about this." And for the next 45 minutes, they had the best business conversation that Carlos had had with anyone in over a year.

Carlos' next two conversations didn't go quite as well as his conversation with Sandra. Both Pamela and James, solid players on Carlos' team, brought something to the meeting for Carlos to Edit. While not as polished or as thorough as Sandra's document, both of the Authored documents allowed for some rich coaching conversations. In both cases, Carlos had the sense that the next time Pamela and James presented Carlos with an Authored document, it was going to be much tighter.

Carlos' last meeting of the afternoon was with one of his more tenured direct reports, Mike. Mike had been with the company for 15 years and had been a Sr. Manager for the last three years. Carlos had heard that Mike had a reputation as a solid contributor when he joined Carlos' team. Up to this point, Carlos had no reason to believe anything different. Mike had always delivered on everything that Carlos had asked him to do.

Carlos' meeting with Mike started off very similarly to his other one-on-ones that afternoon. After he greeted Mike, Carlos invited him over to the table in the corner of his office. But, unlike his other direct reports, Mike didn't reach for a folder or offer anything to Carlos. Instead, Mike just sat there, patiently waiting for Carlos to take control of the meeting.

"Mike, I'm looking forward to our conversation today. As I mentioned in our meeting last week, I'd like to conduct these meetings differently going forward. My expectation is that you will come to every meeting with something 'Authored' for me to 'Edit' and for us to discuss." Carlos paused briefly, then continued. "So, Mike, what would you like to discuss today?"

Mike began to visibly squirm in his seat. This was not going at all as he had hoped. After an awkward silence, Mike started, "Uh, well, I wasn't sure exactly what you were looking for today. I wasn't completely clear on your expectations after our meeting last week. Rather than disappoint you, I thought we could talk about exactly what you would like me to do."

Carlos paused for a moment to reflect on his meeting with Mike the prior week. Had he failed to be clear with Mike? Maybe, after conducting three other Author/Editor conversations, he had gotten tired and missed some key elements in their conversation. Carlos decided that he owed it to Mike to start over.

"Mike, perhaps I didn't do a good job being clear on what I was hoping for out of our conversations going forward. I will own that. Let's start over. I'd like for our conversations to consist more of your unique perspectives and points of view on anything ranging from your team to how we as a department or a business can improve."

When Carlos finished, he calmly made his way back to his desk and after some quick shuffling of papers, retrieved the Authored document that Sandra had provided him earlier this week. He walked back to the table and sat down and continued, "Here is an example of the type of 'Authored' document that I am looking for." Carlos then spent the next few minutes walking Mike through Sandra's document and highlighting the components that he found particularly helpful as the Editor. When Carlos was finished, he excitedly offered, "Mike, why don't I make a copy of this document to take with you? You can use it as you think about what you want to 'Author' for our discussion next week."

Mike nodded in agreement and thanked Carlos for his time. After the meeting, Carlos thought to himself, *Well that went well. I don't know if I could have been more clear.*

A week passed. Carlos had several one-off meetings with members of his team over the course of the week, and he found that those meetings had a new and more productive vibe to them. He found himself reacting to or approving requests rather than dictating next steps. While he was still working long hours at the office, Carlos began to notice that his work after hours at home was starting to let up.

It came time for his weekly one-on-one meetings and like clockwork, Sandra led off the meeting with another solid proposal. In this case, she was recommending creating a new innovative position to solve the growing need for a data analyst on her team. With a quick glance at the budget, Carlos knew it could work and gave Sandra the green light. His meetings with Pamela and James were also noticeably better. While neither of them had something for Carlos to approve, both Pamela and James had taken ownership, displayed initiative, and had shown critical thinking. That was all Carlos asked for.

Then came Carlos' meeting with Mike. Carlos had anxiously anticipated this meeting all week. Unlike his other direct reports, Mike had been oddly quiet since their last meeting. Carlos just assumed that Mike was spending that time preparing an Authored document for their next meeting. When Mike arrived, in typical fashion, Carlos greeted Mike and led him to the small table in the corner. Carlos sat down, clasped his hands in anticipation, and, with a smile, looked at Mike. Mike squirmed slightly and tried to meet Carlos' smile with a forced smile of his own. *Maybe he is just nervous*, thought Carlos.

"Mike, I've been looking forward to our meeting all week," Carlos offered in an attempt to break the silence.

Mike squirmed a bit more and after a few more moments of awkward silence, responded, "Carlos, I've been working hard over the past week to think about what I could prepare for our discussion today. I just didn't want to disappoint you. I thought maybe we could spend our time today with you sharing some of your perspective on my team and department so I can prepare something that would meet your needs. I guess what I'm trying to say is that I could really use your help."

While it wasn't what Carlos was hoping for, of course he couldn't refuse Mike's request for help. Over the next hour Carlos analyzed, dissected, and offered perspective after perspective on Mike's team and portion of the business. At the end of the meeting, Mike stood up, shook Carlos' hand, and thanked him for the additional guidance.

The next week went much like the prior week. A lively and challenging discussion with Sandra offered points of view about the department that Carlos hadn't even considered, continued growth and progress with Pamela and James as they sharpened their Author skills, and largely silence from Mike.

When it again came time for his one-on-one with Mike, Carlos had hoped that the prior week's conversation would help to put Mike on the right track. Carlos' hopes were fueled when Mike sat down and for the first time, pulled out a document and slid it across the table for Carlos to review. As Carlos scanned the document, his excitement slowly faded. Not only had Mike simply tried to copy Sandra's structure, but everything included in the document was exactly what Carlos had said the week prior. There wasn't one unique thought or point of view in the entire report.

Carlos steadied himself before he spoke, "Mike, while I appreciate all of your hard work in putting this together, I was hoping for more of your unique perspectives and views on the business. This simply seems to be a summary of our conversation last week."

Mike tilted his head ever so slightly as if he was hearing something for the first time. "Carlos, I am so sorry. I truly thought this is what you were looking for. I guess I am confused by your expectations."

Ouch. That hurt. Carlos had tried for weeks to make his expectations clear to Mike. By this point, he had run out of ideas. It was time to call in the reinforcements. It was time to call Marilyn.

After ending the meeting with Mike, Carlos picked up the phone and dialed Marilyn's office. Luckily, she answered on the third ring. After a few pleasantries, Marilyn got right to the point, "Carlos, how can I help you?"

Carlos relayed his successes with Sandra, Pamela, and James, but then promptly moved into his struggles and frustrations with Mike. After he outlined the many conversations with Mike and his disappointment with the meeting that afternoon, he stopped and waited for a reply.

"To Author is to be vulnerable," is all Marilyn said. She waited a few moments and repeated the phrase again,

"To Author is to be vulnerable."

Marilyn continued, "Many people would rather have you tell them exactly what you want them to do because as long as they are 'following your orders' they can never be held accountable if things don't go well. What Mike is doing with you is trying to get you to sit in the Author seat so he can sit in the Editor seat. It is a much safer place for him in the long run. He may not get a lot of promotions, but he is unlikely to get fired. And from the looks of it, he has been quite successful in switching the seats on you over the last few weeks."

If Mike's comment earlier in the day had stung, Marilyn's was a punch in the gut. *There is no way I've been sitting in the Author seat with Mike over the last month*, thought Carlos.

"Carlos, I'm sorry. I have to go. I have an evening class of MBA students that I'm teaching tonight. Think about what I said and keep me posted. Good luck." With that, Marilyn ended the call.

Carlos drove home that night still irritated by Marilyn's words. *She couldn't be right*, he thought to himself. He needed to take his mind off of the conversation. Over dinner, his kids suggested watching a movie. It had been so long since Carlos did anything like that on a weeknight. *Why not?* He thought to himself. Maybe it would help him to take his mind off the events of the day.

The kids put in one of their family favorites, Disney's animated version of *Aladdin*. Carlos was just starting to let go of the day as the movie was picking up steam. Aladdin had been stranded in a cave where he met the all-powerful Genie. Upon being released from his magic lamp, the Genie grants Aladdin three wishes to use any way he wants. Not wanting to use one of his precious wishes to get out of the cave, Aladdin comes up with a plan to trick the Genie to rescue him without the use of a wish. Aladdin begins complaining about their situation and that there was no way the genie could be powerful enough to get them out of the cave. The Genie, with his pride on the line, puffs out his chest and with one magical stroke gets them all safely out of the cave.

Once rescued, Aladdin turns to the genie and says, "About my three wishes."

"You are now down to two," responds the Genie.

With a smug look on his face, Aladdin corrects the Genie, "I never asked to be rescued from the cave. You did that on your own."

The genie was stunned. Carlos was stunned. Suddenly he realized the mistake he'd been making with his direct report. Mike had not asked for all of the assistance and help that Carlos presented. It was Carlos who was taking ownership, showing initiative, and displaying critical thinking in their one-on-ones. Not Mike.

Next week, Carlos vowed, was going to be different.

It All Starts with You

The first step in shifting yourself into the Editor seat and moving your team squarely into the Author seat is to communicate these new expectations with your team. I can't emphasize the importance of this first step enough. If you are clear in your expectations, you will not only be able to more effectively shift your natural Authors, but also you will be able to see the resistors more clearly (more on resistors shortly). So, how do you clearly communicate your expectations and what do you need to communicate? Consider the following:

1. Communicate what you are going to <u>stop</u> doing. Naturally, one would start the conversation by talking about the concept of Author vs. Editor. And while that makes for an intellectually stimulating conversation, it isn't going to hit home until you clearly state what you are <u>not</u> going to be doing with and for your team going forward.

Consider the three teenagers that live in my house. One by one, each has complained that "we" (typically one of the parental units) are responsible for somehow damaging their clothes in the weekly process of laundry. We consider this first complaint a "developmental milestone" in our house. Once a kiddo voices the complaint that "we" (the parents) are somehow responsible for their shrunk workout gear or not properly cleaning the ketchup stain from their white t-shirt, they are firmly entrenching themselves in the Editor seat and consequently feel it is quite appropriate to critique the Author on his/her poor laundry skills.

Why is this a developmental milestone you might ask? Because it signals the last time that we will do their laundry for them. Period. From that point forward, they are fully responsible for their own laundry (sorting, washing, rotating, drying, and folding).

As a result, all three of my teenagers have become quite adept at doing their own laundry. Now, this doesn't come without its challenges. Sometimes one kiddo will leave her or his laundry in mid-process for days. Other times, one of them might decide that 1:00 a.m. is the best time to start her or his laundry. That said, we don't have to worry about their ability to do their own laundry in college and beyond.

> *It's amazing what people are capable of when they know what you aren't going to be doing for them.*

Therefore, begin by clearly stating to your team what you are NOT going to be doing for them going forward.

For example:

I'm no longer going to tell you how to solve your specific work-related problems. I will always be here as a sounding board and guide if you want to talk through your challenges, but I won't be writing the plan for you.

I am not going to be telling you what to specifically work on each week. I will always share our department priorities, but what you choose to work on each week in support of those is up to you.

I will no longer be in the details of your team to know who needs a raise or what other resources may be necessary to support your efforts. I will always be open to those conversations and am committed to getting you the resources that you need, but you'll need to bring those to my attention. Don't wait on me.

I will no longer be bringing you and the team my ideas to implement. We'll all need to be engaged in problem-solving, innovation, and brainstorming if we are going to be effective.

2. Communicate what you expect others to <u>start</u> doing. Specifically and most importantly, you can't Edit if your team doesn't bring you something Authored. It is important that you communicate to your team that they need to bring you something to react to during every meeting. This doesn't mean that they have to Author proposals and recommendations every single meeting. It is perfectly appropriate to bring status updates, agendas, and other Authored documents. In essence, it doesn't matter *what* they bring as long as it is clear that they are taking ownership of their role, showing initiative, and displaying critical thinking in what they are bringing you.

<u>For example:</u>

A status update showing all of the current projects as well as what items are on-track, in danger of falling behind, and having issues.

A clear agenda of what she/he would like to discuss with you during the one-on-one. It is okay for this agenda to include clarifying questions for her/his manager.

However, in order for it truly to be representative of an Author, the agenda has to have a clear point-of-view of what the owner believes needs to get accomplished.

A proposal or recommendation for how to improve a process, her/his team, or the business. This should have a logical structure and follow some of the principles that we find in consulting firms.

<u>*Consider the following:*</u>

Situation. *What is the current situation, context, or problem that we might find ourselves in?*

Task. *What are we tasked with accomplishing? What are our priorities that we need to achieve in the current context?*

Action. *What actions are being proposed or recommended? Ideally, there would be two or three options entailing different levels of risk and investment. Pro-tip: Some of the best proposals include a "do nothing" option as well.*

Results. *What is ROI for each recommendation? What are the resource costs for each (investment, time, people, etc...) and likely returns for each?*

3. This is about coaching your Authors to become "*New York Times* bestsellers." Communicate to the team that this isn't about them bringing you the perfect Authored document every time. This approach is designed to not only empower them to take more initiative and ownership on their respective parts of the business, but it is also about having different kinds of weekly conversations. Done well, as the Editor, it allows for you to coach your team on their critical thinking and help them bring their ideas and recommendations to life. It is about you coaching them to improve their work products so they can be "New York Times" bestsellers. Each meeting should be about making them better. Who doesn't want that?

Author vs. Editor Warnings

I hope that at this moment you are thinking to yourself, *this shift sounds so easy and natural.* And for many of our folks, it will be. The natural Authors on your team will relish the permission that you will grant them to put their pen to paper and create something new and beneficial. But there are many ways that the Author/Editor concept can be derailed and short-circuited. Consider the following traps to be avoided:

Warning #1: To Author Is To Be Vulnerable

While many of us love the freedom and responsibility that comes with Authorship, it isn't for everyone. To Author is to be vulnerable. You are putting out your perspectives, points of view, and opinions to your manager. What if she or he doesn't like them? Or worse, what if they dislike them so much that they wonder if you should even be in the role that you are in? For some, the push to be an Author taps into their insecurities. Afterall, they are much safer just doing what you tell them to do. They will think to themselves, *Why can't we just go back to that?*

The good news is that as we move higher up in organizations, resistors to Authoring are less and less common. While you might experience a high percentage of this group in entry level or hourly positions, you are unlikely to encounter many resistors to Authorship in more senior ranks. Afterall, it was Authorship that got them promoted in the first place. That said, it has been my experience that 20% of most direct reports fall into the Resistor category and will fight you every step of the way as you try to push them into the Author seat.

How will you know if you are dealing with a Resistor? You'll know you have encountered a Resistor when you hear any of the following phrases as you try to make the transition:

- *What do you want me to do?*
- *How would you approach this if you were me?*
- *I don't want to disappoint you. Can you tell me exactly what you want to see?*
- *I'm confused...*
- *I don't think I can do this without your help.*

In addition to the above phrases, be prepared to experience bait-and-switch tactics that are sneaky and skillfully deployed. It is important to note that for these Resistors, they have developed some very sophisticated self-protective methods to redirect attention away from themselves in order to keep themselves safe in their jobs and to avoid the feeling of being too exposed.

You will need to be vigilant. These are magicians and tricksters of the highest order. They will find ways to make you think you didn't communicate effectively enough, equip them well-enough, or treat them fairly-enough during your efforts to push them into the Author seat. You may feel guilty. You may begin to second-guess yourself, and soon you could find yourself back in the Author seat allowing them to slip back into the Editor seat. And they will thank you.

But the cost of falling back into old patterns is high. Not only are you unable to fully move from working "in" the business to "on" the business, but you would also be perpetuating a co-dependent relationship and stunting your team member's growth.

Pro Tip: Be diligent, vigilant, and don't be persuaded to backtrack when Resistors push back.

Warning #2: Avoid the Hero Trap

Avoid the "hero" trap. As the manager, it is tempting to be the hero and "rescue" your team when problems emerge. Similar to the prior warning, when we let Resistors persuade us to slip back into the Author seat, when we rescue our teams, we are stunting their growth and creating a co-dependent relationship. This trap is sneaky. We may find ourselves rescuing our team and not even realize we are doing it. It happens to the very best of us.

Some time ago I was retained to speak at a national conference to a group of 15,000 independent auto shop owners. I've always thought you need two trusted service providers in your life: a family doctor and a reliable mechanic. These hard-working auto shop owners do important work to keep things running for all of us—literally. In preparation for this speaking engagement, I had the opportunity to speak with a number of the attendees so I could learn more about their world and day-to-day challenges of their industry. One of my conversations with one of these auto shop owners has stuck with me ever since. This is what he said to me:

> *"You've done all these jobs before. They are easy for you and fun for you. You have gotten out of a mess a million times. And now you see your people are in the same mess. You want to be (and like to be) the hero. But if you want to move yourself to truly being a leader, you need to write a system so others can fix the problem without you."*

Isn't that so spot on? It is not only fun to swoop in and save the day, but you also likely receive applause from your team. But when we do this, we have inadvertently made ourselves the "system." We don't encourage our teams to step up, learn, grow, and "rescue" themselves. But this is hard. Let me offer another story.

Several years ago, I was coaching a senior leader in a large Fortune 500 retailer. With all of my coaching clients, I like to personally conduct 360 interviews with individuals who have worked with her or him in various capacities. I can safely say that this particular set of interviews were some of the most positive that I had ever received about any leader. Interviewees said that people lined up for the opportunity to work with this leader. He was so well respected that many individuals told me that he could be the next CEO if he truly wanted that for his career. Okay, I thought, so he was a great leader. As a coach, that doesn't help me very much. If my role is to make him better, I was going to need something to work with. I pressed and prodded his direct reports. Finally, one of them shared this:

> *"There is one thing he can't do. He doesn't let us fail. When we are working on something and begin to stumble or encounter issues, he swoops in and rescues us. We are all seasoned professionals. We learn best through our failures."*

When I shared this feedback with my client, he looked up at me, shook his head slowly and said, "I'm just not there yet."

Letting others fail is hard. And yes, I know what you are thinking: "Brandon, my organization is running at such full speed that we don't have any room for failure." I get it. In future chapters I will discuss how to use the Author/Editor concept to simulate failures so your team can learn without allowing the business to suffer.

That said, the point is clear. Putting on your cape and rescuing your team will only benefit your ego. In truth, it will cost you time, it will prevent your team from growing, and it will create a co-dependent "system" that will perpetuate until you choose to break it.

Pro-Tip: Next time you feel compelled to swoop in and rescue your team, encourage your team to Author solutions and present them to you to Edit. The world needs more heroes. Help them to experience the pride that comes with solving an urgent problem on their own.

Warning #3: Avoid the Loss of Control Trap

For some managers, letting their direct reports Author can feel like a loss of control. Some of us have a hard time letting go of the "how" with our teams. We not only want our folks to hit all of the goals we set, but we also want them to do it exactly the way that we would do it. And while there are some functions that are bound by certain protocols that may make this necessary (Ex: legal, compliance, accounting, human resources, etc.) in most cases, there are many possible paths to a solution.

Consider the concept of "Commander's Intent" that was referenced earlier to illustrate this point. Several years ago, a retired United States military officer shared this story with me:

> *"After the Iraq War, the U.S. Army realized that the world had gotten too complex. It had become too VUCA (Volatile, Uncertain, Complex and Ambiguous). We couldn't issue those top-down directives that you often see in military movies. We had to go to something called 'Commander's Intent.' The commanding officer would call a meeting with his or her direct reports and their direct reports. During that meeting, the commanding officer would issue the 'Why' of the mission, the 'What' of the mission, and the 'When' of the mission. But they would stay away from the 'How' of the mission because there are too many variables on the battlefield. If everyone leaves*

the meeting clear on the 'Why, What, and When' of the mission, no matter what gets thrown at them, they will move together in an aligned way."

If we are dictating the "How" to our teams, we are taking the Authorship pen out of their hands. In the U.S. Army, they quickly realized this was going to cost the units flexibility, adaptability, and speed. The U.S. Army has another principle they hold dear: *Bias for action.* In short, if we want flexibility, adaptability, and speed, we need to trust our team with the "How" as they execute on our "Commander's Intent."

Pro Tip: Remind yourself that there are many ways to effectively solve a problem. Focus more on your desired results (Commander's Intent) than the process to get there (the "How").

There is no better time to make the shift with your team than today. Start the conversation with them today and watch the natural Authors on your team emerge.

Reflection Questions for You from Chapter 3

- Consider writing down what you want to communicate with your team as you begin to make the shift from Author to Editor.
- What are the actions that you are going to stop doing with your team?
- What are the expectations that you have of your team that you want them to start doing?
- Do you anticipate that you will have any Resistors to Authoring on your team? Why do you think they might be Resistors? What can you do to stay the course and keep yourself firmly in the Editor seat with your direct reports?
- Do you have a tendency to swoop in and rescue your teams? How can you stop yourself and encourage your team to Author solutions in those situations?
- Do you have a difficult time letting go of the "How" with your team? What can you do to trust your team to Author the "How" and still achieve your desired goals?

Chapter 4

Clientele, Don't Clerk

It didn't take Carlos long to reset his approach with Mike. The next day, he called Mike into his office and shared his epiphany. In his attempts to assist Mike, Carlos had inadvertently been doing too much Authoring. He went on to explain that his approach was not helping him or Mike. It wasn't getting Mike any closer to taking ownership, displaying initiative, or showing critical thinking. Carlos concluded the conversation by emphasizing his expectation that all his direct reports needed to be active Authors if the team was to achieve what it was capable of.

Mike didn't take the conversation particularly well, but he realized that Carlos was not going to back down from his position. They agreed that Mike was going to step up his Authoring efforts. As Carlos walked Mike to the door, he didn't want the conversation to feel demoralizing for Mike, so he tried his best to channel his inner Marilyn when he said, "Mike, I know this is uncomfortable for you. I know it feels risky to put yourself out there, but I don't want you to look at it that way. This is a fantastic opportunity for you to not only grow as a leader, but also for our department to benefit from your unique perspectives and ideas."

Carlos waited for a reaction. When Mike didn't respond, Carlos looked at him and simply said, "I believe in you." As Carlos closed the door to his office, he knew he had done everything that he could to put Mike on the right path. Now it was up to Mike.

Over the next few weeks, Carlos' team continued to make progress. Even Mike was showing some signs of improvement. While Carlos was happy with his team's progress, as he looked at hours over the prior few weeks, there was only a gradual improvement. He was still finding himself missing family commitments and working well into the evening.

Every Monday morning, Carlos would meet with his boss, Walter McHenry. Walter was a Vice President and had been with the company for nearly twenty years. Their weekly meetings had the same rhythm each week. Carlos would arrive at Walter's office a few minutes before 10:00 a.m. and, once seated across from his boss, would flip open a yellow legal pad and take notes on everything that came out of Walter's mouth. After each hour-long meeting, Carlos would have a full set of notes and a list of "to do's" to keep him and his team busy for the rest of week and beyond. What was particularly frustrating for Carlos was that in each of these meetings, Walter would present Carlos with a new list of activities different from the prior week's conversation. And every week, the list was more than what Carlos and his team could get accomplished. Carlos felt like he was just trying to keep up.

Carlos' meeting with Walter this week was no different. Walter didn't spend much time on the items that he had identified the prior week, but instead, with the excitement of a kid in a candy aisle, peered over the rims of his glasses and jumped right into new ideas and initiatives. As frustrating as this was for Carlos, he had to admit that Walter had an infectious energy about him which he'd always appreciated.

That said, it was difficult for Carlos to anticipate where he thought Walter might go with the conversation. Sometimes, Walter would want to go deep into the details and ask Carlos specific questions about the smallest of items. For example, one meeting Walter spent nearly the entire meeting wanting to get a handle on the office expenses of the department. By the end of the meeting, Carlos found himself discussing with Walter the number of pens that had been purchased over the last three months. Other times, Walter would want to brainstorm. He would come up with a variety of half-baked ideas that he would expect Carlos to explore during the upcoming week. And then, of course, Walter might want to discuss the projects and initiatives going on in the department.

This week's conversation had a little bit of all three of these elements. Walter opened by wanting a detailed analysis of travel expenses over the last three months. Then he bounced over to some new ideas on how the team could integrate new technology solutions to streamline how they work and share information. This was going to require that Carlos explore some possible options with vendors. Carlos was already dreading those calls and the time it was going to waste. Finally, Walter ended the meeting with a request for updates on several initiatives and requesting that Carlos and the team increase their pace and progress on each initiative. Carlos left the meeting exhausted. He had no idea how he was going to meet all of Walter's demands.

Carlos made it a point to be home for dinner that night. Even though he had plenty of work to do, he knew if he didn't start making family a priority, things with Marisol were only going to get more tense. As they were sitting around the dinner table, Carlos began sharing his frustrations with his meeting with Walter that afternoon. Marisol patiently listened.

After Carlos had sufficiently worn himself out, Marisol responded, "It sounds like you are making great progress with your team, but your relationship with Walter seems to be in the same place it always has been. I don't know exactly how to help you make that shift, but I know someone who might. Why don't you give Marilyn a call? I bet she'd have some advice for you."

Carlos got up from the table, went over to where Marisol was sitting and without saying a word, gave her a gentle kiss on the cheek. "You remind me every day that I am a lucky man to be married to you," Carlos whispered.

After Carlos cleaned up the kitchen and helped get the kids to bed, he picked up the phone and called Marilyn. He updated Marilyn on his efforts with his team and shared his frustrations with his boss. Marilyn peppered him with questions.

Finally, Marilyn responded to what she heard, "Carlos, you have a flow problem. For the 'Author/Editor' concept to work, we must 'Author' up and 'Edit' down. You are Editing down with your team, but you are not Authoring up with your boss. It is clear to me that your boss is doing the 'Authoring' every week. That is the root of your long hours. Meet me at the following address tomorrow at 3:00 p.m. There is someone I would like you to meet."

The next day, Carlos showed up at the address Marilyn had provided him. Carlos double-checked the hastily scribbled address that he held in his hand and then glanced up at the small little boutique in front of where he was parked. Carlos' worries were quickly put at ease when the door to the boutique opened, and a smiling Marilyn waved him into the store.

The inside of the place looked nothing like the store front. It was as if Carlos had been transported into a fashion magazine. The racks and displays held a beautiful assortment of clothing. There were elegant dresses for special occasions, blouses and skirts for every-day wear, t-shirts, jeans, and scarves.

"Carlos, I want to introduce you to the owner of this fine establishment, Sonya Nguyen," said Marilyn.

Sonya appeared from behind one of the displays and immediately the store made sense to Carlos. Sonya looked as if she "was" the store. She had a smooth simple elegance about her. She wore a casual blouse, a pair of faded jeans, and a set of heels that, if you separated them out, weren't particularly special on their own, but combined, was what one might expect to see on a fashion runway. Sonya pulled together the entire look with her dark hair pulled back tightly in an elegant ponytail. While Sonya was only a little over five feet tall, she shared the same energy and presence as Simon.

"Carlos, it is an absolute pleasure to meet a fellow friend and former student of Marilyn," Sonya said as she extended her hand. "Tell me how I may be of assistance?" Sonya asked.

Marilyn smoothly interjected, "Sonya, Carlos is having a 'flow' problem with his manager. He is allowing his manager to 'Author' in every conversation, and it is causing him and his team some major issues. I thought if you could share the story of how you took your boutique from struggling, to competing with some of the more exclusive luxury retailers, to the envy of the fashion world, it would help him tremendously."

While Carlos appreciated a business case study as much as the next person, he was at a loss as to how an entrepreneur's journey was going to help him learn how to better manage his boss. After all, as a business owner Sonya was *the boss*.

Sonya detailed the story of her boutique. Sonya had begun her career in luxury retail, working for a variety of luxury retailers in both store operations as well as corporate. After completing her MBA, she had made the decision to start her own business and opened her boutique.

"In the beginning, I tried too hard to cater to the constantly changing fashions and trends. If a customer asked for it, I would always find a way to get that particular product. Over time, that pressure of maintaining a constantly changing inventory and regularly customizing every request was wearing me out. After a particularly long day at the store, I was standing behind the counter looking over the numbers for the quarter and when I glanced up, I saw the store for what it had become—a complete lack of identity. There were fashion trends from every corner of the globe competing for attention.

"It was then that I remembered something that a retail mentor shared with me years ago: You can get away with Clerking for a while, but the best retailers Clientele. Clerks sit back and say, 'How can I help you?' But when we Clientele with customers, we proactively approach her or him and say, 'you would look amazing in this.' I realized that I had inadvertently established a Clerking culture in my store. And that had to change."

Sonya continued, "You see, I had allowed the customer to be the 'Author' in the relationship. They would come into the store and make requests, and sometimes, those 'Authored' requests were either unreasonable or unrealistic. Yet, I was doing everything I could to try to meet those demands regardless of how practical or possible they might be. Even worse, there were times that those requests were simply not in the best interest of my customer. I knew what they were asking me for wasn't going to give them the look and style they were seeking. Yet, I didn't say anything. I simply took their order. I was not taking ownership, displaying initiative, or, frankly, showing much critical thinking. It was not a very empowering position to be in. I decided that I needed to take back the 'Author' reins and present my customers with what I thought was what they needed. After all, I was the expert."

Sonya shared how she regained control of the identity of her store. She established not only a more clear "point of view" on her style, but also the types of customers that were the ideal fit for her business.

Sonya concluded, "Not only is my store five times more profitable than when I began, but now I have a core group of repeat customers that schedule appointments to meet with me so that I can 'Author' options for them. I intimately know the style and preferences of those customers. That knowledge allows me to pull the items that I know they are going to like prior to their visit. Their trust in my opinions and point of view is so strong that they almost always purchase everything that I recommend. Frankly, it all came down to me shifting to more of a 'clienteling' or 'Author' mindset and I had to stop trying to be all things to all people."

When Sonya had finished her story, Carlos responded, "Sonya, your story is truly impressive. I think every student of business could learn something from you. That said, I'm just not sure how this relates to my challenge with my boss."

A subtle smile appeared on Sonya's face. "Carlos, my challenge with my store is very similar to the challenge you are facing with your manager right now. You see, my 'manager' is my customer. I thought good service was meeting any of my customers' needs and wants. I was wrong. Excellent service is proactively providing guidance and recommendations to my customers based on my knowledge, expertise, and unique point of view. If I was to guess, you are falling into the same trap that I had fallen into. You are probably trying to please your manager by meeting every single little request that he has of you. In reality, he probably doesn't really know what he wants, and more importantly, doesn't understand the implications of his requests on you and your team. I wonder what it would look like if you 'Authored' those conversations more intentionally, putting your manager in the 'Editor' seat. Afterall, according to Marilyn, it sounds like you've been successful making the shift with your team so you know how impactful the shift can be."

Once again, Carlos understood why he held Marilyn in such high regard. Sonya was exactly right. Carlos had been passive regarding his meetings with Walter. He had simply taken Walter's order rather than proactively Author recommendations and bring his point of view to those meetings. An hour later, Carlos left Sonya's boutique with two small bags in his hands. After some skillful questions about Marisol, Sonya had picked out several pieces of jewelry and a beautiful scarf that Carlos simply knew Marisol was going to love.

The following week's meeting with Walter went quite differently. Carlos arrived prepared with a high-level executive summary and proactively led the conversation. He specifically directed Walter to the list of competing initiatives on his team's plate. After some robust discussion, Carlos then guided Walter to a set of choices and options that might create a clearer path forward. In addition, Carlos went one step further and offered his recommendation. In the end, Walter agreed with Carlos and for the first time, Carlos left their weekly meeting feeling focused, energized, and confident that he could achieve everything that they agreed upon before they met again.

He vowed to never relinquish the Author seat with his manager again.

Effectively Authoring Up

Several years ago, I was coaching a client who worked at a consulting firm. He reported directly to one of the managing directors in the firm and had a difficult time each time they met. "I just never know what he wants," he told me. "On top of that, he never asks me any questions about me or my team. I always leave those conversations feeling incredibly unfulfilled." My client had risen through the ranks of the firm because of his exceptional client management skills. He knew how to Author solutions to his clients that they almost always agreed to without much hesitation. After hearing some of his challenges with his managing director, I posed this question to my client:

> *"Rather than viewing your manager as your 'manager,' how might you treat him or her differently if instead you viewed him or her as your number one customer?"*

Upon hearing the question, he just looked at me, stunned. And then it clicked. If he viewed his manager as a client, he would know exactly what to do. He would proactively send status updates on the engagements that his team was actively working through. He would come to every meeting with recommendations and cost/benefit analysis on each. And he would steer his manager in the direction that he thought was best for the firm.

And that was exactly what he did. During our next coaching call, he eagerly gave me the update on his new approach. This is what he told me: "At the end of our meeting, my manager said to me, 'This was the best meeting I've had all week. I felt like I was the client.'"

Just as we want our direct reports to Author up to us so we can Edit, we need to be assuming the Author seat with our managers. When we Author up, not only do we take a more proactive lead in the relationship, but we are also making things more efficient and effective for our manager. We are helping her or him to work more "on" the business rather than "in" the business. By Authoring up, we are ensuring that everyone is sitting in the seat that allows her or him to operate at their highest and best use.

Author vs. Editor Best Practices with Your Manager

There are several best practices that you can start doing today to properly put your manager in the Editor seat. Consider the following:

1. Treat your manager as your number one customer. This is a simple shift, but perhaps the most important one that you can make. From this point forward, never view your manager as your manager. View him or her as your number one customer. When you do that, it immediately activates your "client management" skills. You become more intentional in providing proactive updates and communication. You regularly check in to ensure that they are getting their needs met. You actively try to manage the "scope" of the project to ensure you and your team don't exceed the agreed upon resources. And you do all of this with a positive attitude.

Treat your manager as your number one customer and see how it changes the dynamic.

2. Clientele with your manager; never Clerk. Several years ago, I was working with a luxury retailer. During the time of my engagement with them, e-commerce had significantly disrupted this retailer's business. As one long-term leader in the business shared with me, "We used to view ourselves as merchants. We took pride in being purveyors of fine goods. Customers would come to us to get some of the finest and most elegant merchandise anywhere. E-commerce completely disrupted that. Now customers can get anything they want sent to them. As a result, we needed to give them a reason to come to our store. We could no longer sit back and Clerk when a customer came in. When we Clerk, we sit back passively and say, 'how can I help you?' We needed to learn to Clientele. When we Clientele we proactively walk up to a customer and say, 'You would look amazing in this.'"

Similar to the first best practice, we should not take a reactive role with our manager. When we assume a Clerking role with our boss, we put her or him in the Author seat. Not only does this keep us in a reactive mode, but it prevents us from having any say or control over what our manager may ask for (or how reasonable her or his request may be, for that matter). When we Clientele, we assume the Author role and present our manager with multiple options for them to choose from. (Note: three is a good target number of options.) Not only do they appreciate being in the Editor seat, but it also provides us considerable control over the menu of options, thus preventing unreasonable or unrealistic requests.

3. Always be prepared to bring a "point of view" to meetings with your manager. As an executive coach for well over 15 years, I have done my fair share of 360-degree interviews on behalf of my clients. I have coached clients ranging from managers to C-level executives across every possible vocation imaginable, from rocket scientists to prison wardens.

Over the years, I've seen many common patterns emerge. One of those patterns is the difference between the manager role and the director role. As one senior leader from a tech company shared with me, "When you become a director, we expect you to always bring your point of view to meetings. As a manager, this is a nice-to-have, but not a requirement. For director-level and above, bringing your point-of-view to meetings is a necessity."

"Bringing your point of view" is another form of Authorship. When we formulate a position, clarify a goal, or identify challenges, we demonstrate our ownership, show initiative, and display critical thinking. From this point forward, when preparing for meetings with your manager, be intentional to share your point of view. This could be as simple as sharing your answers to the following questions:

a. What is working well?
b. What is not going as expected?
c. What should we be monitoring going forward?

You'll notice, unlike with "clienteling," when we offer our point of view, we aren't necessarily offering a solution. Perhaps, it is too early for a solution. That said, we are actively taking ownership, showing initiative, and displaying critical thinking when we proactively analyze a situation.

Consider the following example. Imagine you oversee a chewing gum plant. You and your team produce over 50% of all chewing gum bought across North America. Your plant has always been profitable, with steady orders and a high growth rate year-over-year. The pandemic hits in 2020 and your orders begin to tumble. Strangely enough, your product is particularly hard hit compared to your sister candy plants (Ex: chocolates, hard candies, etc.). It is early in the pandemic, so you aren't ready to make any drastic changes. However, keeping an eye on the situation will be critical as the pandemic continues to disrupt the business in very unpredictable ways. How might you communicate your point of view with corporate so they are aware of the situation and you are guiding them on possible remedies to the situation?

Sometimes, it is just too early for solutions, but it is never too early for ownership, initiative, and critical thinking. By the way, if you haven't guessed it, the reason why chewing gum took a hit in 2020 was because consumers chew gum when they go out in public and meet other people in social settings. They don't want to have bad breath in that client meeting or on that first date. In 2020, the only people we were seeing were our own families. Apparently, based on chewing gum purchases in 2020, we decided that we didn't care if our families had to endure our bad breath.

Unfortunately, the best practices above are not typically applied by most of the professionals that I have encountered over the years. They simply sit in the wrong seat with their leaders. Let me share some of the missteps that I see commonly made.

Author vs. Editor Traps We Fall into With Our Manager

Trap #1: We assume that if we Clerk well with our manager, she or he will be happy with us. We "order take" and try to meet all of our manager's requests. While this sounds logical, consider this analogy. Imagine you were a server in a restaurant. Here is the catch: There is no menu. Your job is to take the order of your customer and then get it filled, regardless of the request. Imagine the kind of chaos that would ensue when your customer ordered steamed dumplings, a hamburger, kale salad, squid ink tagliatelle, and an entire German chocolate cake. Other than questioning your patron's caloric consumption, you would be running frantically to get all of the ingredients necessary to fulfill her or his request.

Naturally, a limited and focused menu would solve this issue and ensure that not only could we meet our customer's requests, but also it would likely be something we could deliver in a very efficient and skilled way. (Note: If you have ever watched one of those "restaurant rescue" shows, you'll notice that refining and tightening the menu is one of the first changes that is made.) Again, the key here is to be able to Author the options that are available to your manager in advance.

Trap #2: We assume our manager knows what she or he needs and wants and knows the best way to get it. Just like with customers, it is easy to confuse needs and wants. Perhaps your manager has the need to impress her or his manager. So, they come to you and ask you to cut all of your project timelines in half, creating mass chaos and pressure on you and your team. Had we known that their ultimate goal was to impress their manager, perhaps we could have come up with another solution to achieve that goal.

Trap #3: We assume our manager knows what is on our (or our team's) plate. We tend to assume that our manager remembers all of the requests that they have made of us over the last month and is keeping a ledger, sensitively trying to make sure they don't break us with the volume of their requests. The reality is that they are likely just pushing down demands that have come from their manager. They are looking at their plate and asking themselves "Do I want to do this?" and "Do

I have capacity for this?" If the answer is "No" to either, guess what? You have a new item added to your plate. Because your manager does not recall what's on your list already, it will be your duty to Author reminders to them with regular communications and status updates.

Trap #4: **We assume our manager is focused on our needs and wants.** Similar to Trap #3, we tend to assume that our manager is spending time thinking about our needs and wants. The reality is that they are more focused on their "customer"—their manager. It is up to us to communicate what we need and want in order to be effective in delivering on our manager's requests. It is when we expect our manager to know and act on our needs and wants that we become disappointed and resentful. We would never expect that of a customer so why do we expect that same behavior from our manager? Therefore, it is imperative that you Author requests for resources required to meet the goals of your team.

In summary, if you apply the above best practices with your manager and avoid the more common traps, not only will you properly keep the Author/Editor flow moving in the right direction (remember, we Author Up) but you will also realize the following benefits:

- More productive and focused meetings with your manager
- Fewer unrealistic, unreasonable, or poorly timed demands from your manager
- Enhanced trust and empowerment from your manager as she or he becomes more comfortable serving in the Editor seat
- Improved performance review ratings and a higher probability that you are seen as an "emerging leader" in the organization

- More influence over your and your team's workload resulting in less feelings of overwhelm, anxiety, and burnout
- Both parties are sitting the seats that allow her or him to be at their highest and best use

Who doesn't want those outcomes? I think you know what you need to do. Get started Authoring with your manager today.

Reflection Questions for You from Chapter 4

- Do you fall into any of the following traps with your manager?
    - o Do you assume that if you Clerk well with your manager, she or he will be happy with you?
    - o Do you assume your manager knows what she or he needs and wants?
    - o Do you assume your manager knows what is on your (or your team's) plate?
    - o Do you assume your manager is focused on your needs and wants?
- Do you treat your manager as your number one customer? If yes, how? If not, what could you begin doing to move toward that behavior?
- Do you Clientele with your manager and proactively provide your manager with suggestions, options, and recommendations?
- Do you proactively bring a "point of view" to meetings with your manager?
- In what ways would you like to improve the way you interact with your manager?

CHAPTER 5

To Edit Is to Coach

IT WAS NOW the Fall of 2002. Several months had passed since Carlos had implemented his new approach to meetings with Walter, and things couldn't have gone smoother. By the third meeting with the new approach, Walter had become so accustomed to the Editor role, that he started opening every meeting by asking Carlos, "So, what do you have for me today?" Better yet, Carlos was leaving these meetings with clearer and more manageable expectations for the week. It was helping his team focus in a way that they never could before.

And speaking of his team, while Mike still had some occasional slips, the team had truly embraced the Author role with Carlos. Projects were getting accomplished at a rate that Carlos had never experienced with this team or any of his prior teams. Most importantly, Carlos was finding himself home for dinner almost every night.

Carlos' progress did not go unnoticed by his peers. Every Wednesday morning, Walter would hold a team meeting with all of his direct reports which consisted of Carlos and four other directors. The tipping point was a Wednesday morning meeting where Walter singled out every one of his direct reports and went deep into the weeds, noticeably excluding

Carlos from this treatment. As Carlos was packing up his briefcase, he was approached by two of his peers, Allen and Cynthia.

Trying not to be too obvious, Allen leaned over to Carlos and casually whispered, "Carlos, would you have time to meet with Cynthia and me for lunch today? We've noticed a distinct change in how you are managing your team, and Walter for that matter. We'd love to pick your brain."

Carlos looked up from his briefcase with a smile and said, "Of course. I'd be happy to meet."

At noon that day, the three of them met at a restaurant a few blocks from the office. As they sat down at the table, Cynthia cut straight to the point, "Okay Carlos. Spill it. What have you been doing that has gotten Walter off of your back? I've been on his team for almost four years, and I've never been able to get him to focus, let alone give me and my team realistic expectations. It seems like every week he has something new for us, and frankly it is burning us out."

Over the next two hours, Carlos recounted his journey from struggling leader to applying the principles of Author vs. Editor with his team and Walter. He shared his many conversations with Marilyn, the struggles he had shifting his team, and finally, his new proactive approach with Walter. Allen and Cynthia were alternating between hastily taking notes and peppering Carlos with questions.

As the three of them left the restaurant, Allen spoke, "I can't speak for Cynthia, but this conversation was a 'game-changer' for me. Would you be willing to meet with me once a week as I begin to make these shifts with my team? It would be tremendously helpful to me to have someone who has already made the shifts to bounce ideas off of."

Without waiting for Carlos' response, Cynthia chimed in, "I echo everything Allen just said. Count me in." Carlos happily agreed.

From that day forward, every Friday the three directors met at that same restaurant for lunch to discuss implementing Author vs. Editor with their teams. The first week was as Carlos had predicted. Both Cynthia and Allen had several members of their teams that readily accepted the role of Author. They also had a few resistors. Luckily, Carlos prepared them for the likelihood of resistance from his experience working with Mike, so they knew what signs to look out for. Progress remained steady the second week as Cynthia and Allen deliberately began shifting their teams into the Author seat.

By week three, things started taking a different turn. After they sat down for their Friday lunch meeting and placed their orders, Cynthia began, "I'm concerned that my team is starting to revolt against the role of 'Author.' Most concerning, I'm getting some passive aggressive resistance from the members of my team that embraced the 'Author' role the quickest. I'm not sure what that is about."

Carlos thought for a moment and responded, "Passive aggressive? Cynthia, what do you mean?"

With an exasperated sigh, Cynthia said, "After my last meeting with Maryam, my top performer, she asked if we could go back to our prior meeting format. She went on to explain that it was much better for her to have me tell her exactly what I wanted. She was the first one to jump on the 'Author' band wagon."

Carlos hadn't experienced that type of push-back with his team. He was curious as to what might be triggering such a reaction. He pulled out a pad of paper and then asked, "That does sound frustrating. Can you tell me what a typical meeting looks like?"

Cynthia began to detail the flow of each meeting with her direct reports. "Just as the three of us have discussed, the meeting starts with each of my direct reports presenting me with something that they have

'Authored' for us to review. We then cover each point in detail, and I offer coaching and advice. They leave the meeting with action items based on our discussion. Here, I have a copy of one of the 'Authored' recommendations from this week that I have 'Edited.' This particular document was prepared by Maryam. While this is Maryam's document, in an effort to make things easier for my team, I have instructed them to all use the same 'Authoring' format that I prepared for them."

Carlos reached out and took the document from Cynthia. What he immediately noticed was all of the red on the first page. Cynthia had marked up every point that she felt was either incorrect, inaccurate, or wanted to amend. As Carlos flipped through the document, he asked Cynthia, "Are you marking up all of your team's documents like this?"

"Well, yes. Per our discussion, as I understand it, the role of the 'Editor' is to help elevate the 'Author's' critical thinking. I mark up anything that may need some discussion in an effort to get them critically approaching their work the way that I would want them to."

Carlos paused for a few moments as he continued to review the document and take in what Cynthia was telling him. "And have you seen any progress with your team since you started this approach? Or, in other words, are you using any less 'red' week over week?"

Cynthia thought for a moment, and responded, "Well, I guess it is about the same. In some cases, I've actually found myself using more 'red' in the cases in which they are proposing something more creative or ambitious."

Cynthia's rationale made sense to Carlos, and yet he couldn't figure out why things were starting to turn for Cynthia. He ended the meeting telling her he would think about it over the weekend and see if he had any good solutions for her dilemma.

Carlos thought about Cynthia's challenge all weekend but couldn't make any sense of it. It seemed she was doing everything that he had been taught. She was making her expectations clear for every meeting. She was focusing her time in the meetings on trying to elevate the critical thinking of her team. She was providing feedback. What was missing?

It was 7:00 on Sunday night. After thinking about Cynthia's situation and having not made substantial progress regarding a possible solution, Carlos reached for the phone. "This is Marilyn," said the voice on the other line.

It had been a few months since Carlos and Marilyn had spoken. After catching Marilyn up on all of his personal progress with his team and Walter, he shared with her his new role of "teacher" for his peers as they attempted to implement Author vs. Editor with their teams. He detailed the challenge that Cynthia was having with her team. When he finished giving Marilyn all the background from his conversation with Cynthia, he paused and waited for her response. As usual, he didn't have to wait long.

"Carlos, there is a big difference between being an 'Editor' and being a 'critic'. 'Editors' coach. They provide positive feedback and look to refine what the 'Author' brings to them. They aren't looking to break-down, beat-down, or shape the 'Author' into a carbon copy of themselves. Effective 'Editors' use the principle from improv theater of 'yes, and' with their 'Authors.' They look to build on the momentum that their 'Authors' are creating by saying 'yes, and' versus saying 'no, but.'

"Critics, on the other hand, primarily use negative feedback to affect change. They have a tendency to look for what is wrong, inaccurate, or 'off the mark' first and go directly there. Critics look for the little things that are out of place rather than all of the good things that are right where they need to be. Critics correct while 'Editors' shape. Critics critique while 'Authors' coach. Critics demoralize while 'Authors' inspire."

Of course, thought Carlos. All the red ink should have been a give-away. If he had put himself in the position of one of Cynthia's direct reports, he would have begun to feel the same way after the third meeting of getting all of his ideas "marked up." It would have been very frustrating and demoralizing. After thanking Marilyn once again, Carlos hung up and was looking forward to sharing the feedback with Cynthia the next day.

The next morning, Carlos didn't waste any time. As soon as got to the office, he walked directly to Cynthia's office and got there just as she was arriving. "Cynthia, I had a very enlightening call with Marilyn last night, and I think I know what your challenge has been." Carlos summarized his conversation with Marilyn, and when he finished, Cynthia had a perplexed look on her face.

"I just don't understand," she said. "If what I was doing was not coaching, then what is coaching? I'm not sure what I'm supposed to do now."

Carlos thought for a moment about his style with his team, and with a smile, he offered the following, "I think I've got an idea. Try this approach instead with your team when they bring you something that they have 'Authored.' Step one is to first look for what you like. What is directionally correct or something that you are pleased with? Discuss that first. If you do have to make any amendments, try what Marilyn mentioned to me last night. Use the principle from improv of 'yes, and' when giving feedback. Acknowledge what is good about what they are proposing and then say, 'This is really good, and what we could do to make it work would be to make the following minor amendments.' Finally, when the meeting is done, share your appreciation for what they brought to you, so they feel motivated to do it again next week."

Cynthia thought for a few moments and nodded her head slowly in agreement looking slightly embarrassed. "Carlos, that sounds so obvious, and yet, if I was gut-level honest, I haven't been doing any of those things in these meetings. I've been critiquing when I should have been coaching."

A few weeks passed and Carlos, Allen, and Cynthia met again for one of their Author vs. Editor lunches. Cynthia started the meeting with a big smile and offered to pay for everyone's meal. "Carlos, I've been making the changes that you and I discussed, and yesterday was the best meeting I've ever had with Maryam. She brought in some truly brilliant ideas on how we could cut costs while improving productivity. I honestly thought she was going to give me a hug before she walked out the door. The team is truly firing on all cylinders."

After Cynthia finished giving her update, Allen gingerly chimed in, "I don't mean to ruin the good mood, but I'm actually having some challenges of my own with my team. During the first month of shifting the team into the 'Author' seat, my team was very motivated and inspired to 'Author.' I was trying to empower them during every opportunity. But this week, they've been coming to me with more frustrations and complaints rather than enthusiasm, or frankly progress."

Carlos responded to Allen's update, "I'm sorry to hear that, Allen. Can you give me a little more detail and insight into how your weekly one-on-one meetings play out? Just like with Cynthia, that might help us see some opportunities to right the ship."

"Sure," responded Allen. "Just like we discussed, my team would bring me their ideas. I would tell them how great they were, and I empowered them to put them into action as is. I would say, 'This looks great. I'm really impressed. You have my blessing to take ownership and show initiative. Go implement this.' Well, after a few weeks, it turned out that some of the ideas were in conflict with other ideas from the members of the team. For example, one team member proposed that we hire someone to be a project manager for the department, while another team member proposed buying a software package that would accomplish the same goal. In my meetings with each of them, I gave them the green light to proceed, but when they ran into each other trying to accomplish the same goal, they didn't know what to do."

"So, what did you do when they brought this to your attention?" responded Carlos.

Allen continued, "Well, I told them that I expected them to work together and collaborate on finding a solution. I even suggested that they take the idea of 'Author versus Editor' and one team member could 'Author' a solution for the other team member to 'Edit.'"

Carlos thought for a moment and responded, "That sounds reasonable. How did they respond?"

Allen started shaking his head back and forth vigorously. "Let me tell you, it didn't turn out well at all. It started with continued push-back on me to make a decision. The more I pushed for them to work it out, the greater the tension. On top of that, I think putting them in 'Author' and 'Editor' seats with each other just made things worse. I now have several team members that aren't speaking with each other, and I'm starting to hear the same thing that Cynthia was hearing from her team. They are done with the 'Author Editor' thing and just want me to tell them what to do."

As Carlos took a bite from his sandwich, he remembered a quote that Marilyn had on one of her slides in class. It simply said, "Delegation Does Not Mean Abdication." At the time, he didn't know what she meant, but this situation with Allen was putting that in perspective. Allen wasn't actually making decisions or coaching his team. He was simply approving everything they brought him and was telling his team to work it out amongst themselves. Unlike Cynthia who was micromanaging and stifling her team, Allen was doing the exact opposite. He was taking his hands off the steering wheel and walking away. Marilyn used to always say that "Empowerment can't exist without accountability." Perhaps this was the answer.

Carlos finished his sandwich and eased back into the dialogue and asked a few clarifying questions of his own. Upon further discovery, not only was Allen avoiding any type of accountability, but also, he wasn't setting clear expectations or parameters for his 'Authors' to align towards. Luckily, these were some of Cynthia's strengths. She saw exactly where things were going and she jumped right in with gusto, offering Allen some solid tips and strategies for balancing empowerment with accountability.

When the lunch ended, Allen couldn't stop talking. Not only was he motivated to try out the new approaches, but he was also asking Cynthia for more pointers on how to drive greater clarity with his team. Thrilled as Carlos was for Allen's progress, it was clear to Carlos that Cynthia was truly getting the concept of Author vs. Editor. There was just one thing that was still bothering him. He didn't understand why things took a turn for the worse when Allen encouraged his team to use the technique with each other.

Things progressed well for Allen and Cynthia over the next month. Not only were their teams embracing the Author role, but so were Allen and Cynthia in their interactions with Walter. The Friday lunches continued, but the conversations shifted to other topics as everyone at the table was not only getting more accomplished in less time but also were having more time to focus on things that really mattered, like the overall business and their families.

Before Carlos knew it, his annual "guest lecturing date" for Marilyn's Evening MBA class was upon him. He always looked forward to that night. It was a great way for him to give back and reminisce about his time as a student in Marilyn's class. This particular year, he approached his time a little differently. In addition to sharing his professional journey and answering questions about his industry, he made it a point, with Marilyn's permission, to share his experience with the Author vs. Editor concept and how it transformed his leadership approach with his team.

It was during Q&A with the students that Carlos got the question he had been wrestling with for months. A student raised his hand and to Carlos' dismay, asked the following: "I've got a peer that I would like to collaborate with more effectively. Do you think the 'Author versus Editor' tool could help?" Carlos was stumped. This was a question he wasn't ready to answer. Luckily, before he could reply, Marilyn responded from her seat in the back of the classroom.

> *"The 'Author versus Editor' framework works elegantly in ANY vertical relationship. From managing your manager, to leading your team. From influencing clients to parenting, it can be applied in any vertical relationship with success."*

She quickly clarified: "That said, it is NOT a lateral tool. If you use it with peers, you will inadvertently create a power dynamic. One person feels like she or he has more power because they can sit in the 'Editor' seat and has permission to assign a peer to 'Author' something for her or his review."

After Marilyn concluded her thought, the student followed-up, "Is there any way to use it in those settings? It just seems it has the power to reach good outcomes if leveraged properly."

Marilyn, thought for a moment and answered, "Yes. It can be used as a collaborative tool if both parties <u>Author together</u> and then <u>Edit together</u>. They have to sit in the same seat at the same time."

And there it was. *That's why Allen's team imploded!*, thought Carlos. Allen had inadvertently created a power struggle. He'd make a note to tell Allen and Cynthia at their next lunch. Don't use Author vs. Editor as a lateral tool unless both parties sit in the same seat at the same time.

After the last student had left, Carlos, exhausted and invigorated from the class, thanked Marilyn for her wisdom, and walked out to his car. As he made his way through the parking lot, there was something Marilyn said in her answer that was still knocking around in his head. *"From influencing clients to parenting, 'Author versus Editor' could be applied in ANY vertical relationship."* Marilyn said "parenting." He wondered what she meant by that...

―――◦―――

Good Coaching Is Rare

My middle child, Noah, absolutely fell in love with baseball. He would find ways to go outside and practice by himself at every opportunity that he could. From throwing, to hitting, to sliding, he would be outside for hours. He had big dreams of continuing on with baseball for many years with hopes of even playing in college one day.

But there was a problem. Noah didn't pick up his first baseball until he was 12 years old. Where we live in the United States, that is eight years too late, or more appropriately, sixteen seasons too late. Noah had a big hill to climb if he wanted to catch up with his contemporaries, and there were going to be a lot of obstacles in his way. Unbeknownst to us, one of the major obstacles was going to be his coaches.

Noah started his baseball endeavors in recreational baseball (affectionately called "rec ball"). These are typically community-based baseball leagues that are open to anyone of any skill level. Of course, it is equally open to any coaches of any skill level. In rec ball, you are likely to experience the same range of coaches as you do players. Typically, these coaches are dads of players in the league. Some of these coaches come with years of experience, and some are new to the game. Some are insistent on winning at all costs and some are those whose primary objective is to have fun and allow kids the opportunity to take risks.

Rec ball treated Noah well. He was afforded ample playing time and saw some significant improvements over his first four seasons. He had coaches that worked with him on everything from the basics of throwing to more advanced skills at the catcher position. Overall, these coaches were positive and affirming.

Then we were introduced to "travel baseball." For those unfamiliar, this is the perverse business evolution of most youth sports in America where a parent drops several thousands of dollars a season so that every night (as well as the weekends) is spent shuttling your child to practice and tournaments. (Yes, I am not a fan of travel sports for many reasons, but that is for another day.) Noah was invited to be on one of these teams. The level of competition increased, and he started to see improvements in his game.

However, there were two big issues. First, the coaches gave him very little playing time in the actual games. It is a little hard to improve your abilities at the catcher position when you are not given the opportunity to actually catch. Second, and just as importantly, the coaches did not provide much feedback. They didn't "coach" much at all to the players on an individual basis. Instead, they would typically walk around during practices and shout out generalities to the entire team (Ex: "Runner on second. Two outs. Where's the play?"). They rarely if ever pulled a player aside and actually provided any positive reinforcement, guidance, or advice. Noah had one particular travel coach who was fond of one-hour, post-game lectures where he proceeded to berate the team on all of the mistakes they made, not acknowledging any of the positives.

Noah tried not to let that deter him. He would approach his coaches either during or after practice and ask for how he could improve. He was not afraid to ask what it would take for him to get an opportunity to get more playing time. They responded positively to his Authored approach, but at the end of the day, they never followed through with their promises.

After a particularly disappointing travel baseball season where he found himself spending full weekends sitting on the bench watching his team play and not getting any playing time despite his efforts and the coaches' hollow promises, Noah had had enough. He hung up his cleats, put up his baseball equipment and hasn't touched them since. The passion he had for the game had been sufficiently extinguished by the very individuals that should have nurtured his efforts.

Fast-forward a year. As a 16-year-old with an old truck that requires expenses, he took the initiative and picked up a job working at Jersey Mike's (a quick service sandwich franchise) making sub sandwiches. He works long shifts (ten to 12 hours on the weekends) dealing with unruly, demanding, and sometimes irrational customers.

After a particularly long shift, my wife asked Noah, "Do you like working?"

Noah replied, "Absolutely. I get appreciated and recognized for the effort I put in. It's a lot of fun."

Coaching Makes All the Difference

Take the case of Noah. Here is a kid who was extremely passionate about baseball and was actively seeking opportunities to learn and grow. He insisted on being the first to baseball practice, was always looking for opportunities to learn from his coaches, and took initiative at home without being told to do so. He was typically the only kid on his team that would actively ask the coach what more he needed to do to improve. In return, he received vague responses (And on more than one occasion, broken promises. Ex: "I promise to put you in the next game."), little affirmation of his efforts, and no opportunity to Author (play in the game). When there was feedback given, it was delivered as criticism, not as coaching. The net result? Noah would rather earn minimum wage making sandwiches for ten hours straight than step foot on another baseball diamond to play a game.

Perhaps the most important question in this story is this:

What kind of coach are you?

Editor as a Coach: Coaching Best Practices

There are several simple best practices that can move you from ineffective to impactful coach. Consider the following:

1. Start by looking for and acknowledging what you like. This simple best practice is your starting place as a coach. Rooted in positive psychology, and proven to have strong ties with change, start by looking for what you see working in what your direct report has Authored for you. This is not puffery. This serves a very important purpose. You are reinforcing what they did that worked so they continue to do that same thing next time. Thus, when you provide redirecting feedback, they are layering on top of what is working, rather than guessing each and every time. Over the course of multiple Author/Editor meetings, your direct reports will start to learn your style and preferences. Soon, you'll find your Edits become less and less. Consider starting your coaching conversations this way:

a. "Here are the elements that you nailed in this..."
b. "Let's talk about what you have presented today that is strong, and more importantly, why it is so strong (or effective)..."
c. "I really like how you..."

2. Use the technique from improv theater and say, "Yes/And." In the spirit of building on, we are going to take a page from our friends in the improv theater space and approach our coaching feedback with a "yes/and" approach versus a "no/but" approach. If you aren't familiar with improv theater, the actors riff off of each other as they co-Author and co-construct a humorous story. Often the audience is allowed to throw out ideas that the actors are compelled to incorporate into their storyline, regardless of how ridiculous they may be (Ex: You are a dinosaur couple and as a meteor is rapidly approaching Earth, your mother-in-law comes to visit...). The actors can never say "no/but." Their number one rule is that they have to maintain the momentum of the story by saying "yes/and." As a coach, you too must maintain the momentum of the Authored work. Consider saying "yes/and" when you want to make Edits. Any of these sentence stems may be of help:

a. "This is very strong. What would take this to the next level would be..."
b. "I like where you are going with this. If we want to consider additional perspectives from the business, you could add..."
c. "You have considered many critical elements in your thinking. This would be air-tight if you added..."

3. Clearly state and restate the priorities with the team and work to align to those in your coaching. As an important reminder, it is our job as managers and leaders to regularly ensure focus and alignment of the team. This reinforces and supports the idea of communicating your "commander's intent" with your team. As we've reviewed in prior chapters, the Editor needs to communicate her or his commander's intent (the "why, what, and when" of the mission). But that is not enough. When presented with ideas and recommendations, you must reflect and compare those to your commander's intent to not only reinforce your priorities but also to ensure your team "gets it" and is aligning toward those. Consider using the following in your conversations:

a. "Here are all the ways that you have aligned with goals that I've laid out with the team..."
b. "As you think about our priorities, in what ways do you see your recommendation helping us to achieve those goals?"
c. "Here is where you were very consistent with the direction that we are heading in. In addition, here are a few other possible constraints to consider that might impact what you are recommending..."

4. End the conversations by motivating and inspiring your team. When you end your conversation with your team, make sure you are leaving them on a positive, or more importantly, an inspiring, note. Several years ago, I recall listening to a talk given by the Stanford professor, Bob Sutton. At the end of the talk, he was taking questions from the audience, and he shared a story. He referenced a group of consultants doing research around what makes an effective manager. As they were putting together their survey, at the last moment, they came up with what they thought was a "throw-away" question: "When you leave your manager's office, how do you feel?" Turns out, the answer to that question had the highest correlation to managerial effectiveness. It didn't mean that every conversation with one's manager was "happy." But what it did mean was that direct reports of those most effective managers left the conversation with more energy than they entered. They felt motivated, encouraged, or inspired to continue to press forward. Good coaches leave their coachees feeling that way. Consider using the following inspirational phrases as you end your coaching conversations:

a. "I believe in you..."
b. "I see something in you that you don't see in yourself..."

c. "I know you are capable of more..."
d. "I'm proud of you. Keep up the great work..."

Author vs. Editor Traps We Fall into When Editing (Coaching) Our Team

This chapter highlights the important role of the Editor as a coach. That said, we have some new Author vs. Editor traps to explore and to avoid.

> **Trap #1: We confuse Editing with criticism.** It can be a slippery slope between providing some redirecting feedback and moving into full-on critic mode, red-lining most things that our direct reports Author for us.
>
> When I think of a critic, my mind naturally goes to the character of Ego from the Pixar movie, *Ratatouille*. If you haven't seen the movie, I encourage you to make the time. It is a masterpiece for many reasons. But for our purposes here, Ego, the food critic, is feared for his scathing criticisms of any aspiring chef. He dares them to bring him their very best, with the high likelihood that they will be utterly destroyed in the next edition of his column. He despises being directly challenged, and perversely enjoys the process of criticizing more than the actual enjoyment of the delicious meals presented to him by some of the very finest chefs. In short, don't be Ego.
>
> Our job is to encourage and refine. Not break-down and destroy. In addition, when we criticize, we are actually making the entire conversation about elevating ourselves by pushing down others (like Ego).

Trap #2: **In an effort to be supportive, we abdicate or avoid all direction and feedback.** Think of this trap as the other end of the spectrum from Trap #1. Rather than being seen as a micromanager or a critic, we simply say, "Great job," and move on to the next thing. This can also result in frustration as over time, our direct reports aren't getting any type of guidance on how to improve. Worse, this can come across as uncaring or pandering because we aren't being perceived as investing the time to actually provide any real feedback. If this style of coaching is consistent across the team, inevitably, there will be clashes of ideas, initiatives, and priorities. It is a good reminder for us that one of the jobs of a manager and leader is alignment. When we Edit effectively, we are not only providing feedback for individual improvement but also, we are ensuring alignment with all members of the team.

By following the coaching best practices outlined above and avoiding the common traps, not only can you elevate your coaching skills, but more importantly, you can encourage your team to embrace their role as active and proactive Authors. The last thing we want to see is our team "hang up their cleats" because we didn't encourage their ownership, initiative, and critical thinking.

Reflection Questions for You from Chapter 5

- When have you found yourself falling into the trap of being a "critic" with members of your team? How did they respond?
- Are there times you have found yourself too willing to just simply agree with your direct reports' Authored ideas rather than offering critical feedback? What do you think that cost your team? What do you think it cost you?
- Do you start meetings with your direct reports by looking for what is working in order to build momentum? If not, what would it look like if you opened meetings in that way?
- Do you practice a "Yes, and" approach with your direct reports as a form of delivering critical feedback?
- Are you restating and aligning your coaching conversations with your "commander's intent" to ensure focus and alignment of your direct reports' Authored ideas?
- Are you intentionally ending your coaching conversations with an inspirational "call to action?"

CHAPTER 6

Authoring and Editing at Home

THE WEEKEND SNUCK up on Carlos. He had been so busy helping his peers and preparing for his guest lecture for Marilyn's class that he had lost track of the days. That said, it was a Saturday morning in the Fall of 2002. Carlos was lying in bed, staring up at the ceiling. He didn't know what to do with himself. For the first time in years, Carlos did not feel any compelling reason to go into the office on the weekend. He was caught up, and in the areas that they might still need some catching up to do, Carlos knew his team had everything under control. In addition, he had fallen into a very healthy rhythm with Walter and had already prepared his talking points for their next one on one meeting the upcoming week. Carlos could actually dedicate the entire weekend to his family.

Thirty minutes later, Carlos was sitting down at the kitchen table talking. As Marisol prepared breakfast, Carlos took a sip of his coffee and admired how smoothly and effortlessly Marisol operated. "So, what are we going to do today?" he asked Marisol.

"Don't you remember? Jose has a baseball game this morning at 10:00 a.m. He'll need to get to the baseball field at 9:00 a.m. so we'll need to get going pretty soon," replied Marisol. Carlos was kicking himself.

He should have remembered that Jose had a game that morning; Jose had games every Saturday morning during the baseball season. Jose was 12 years old and had been playing baseball for the last five years. Averaging two seasons a year, this was Jose's tenth baseball season. As Carlos thought about it, he wondered if Jose truly enjoyed playing or if he was just going through the motions.

"I completely forgot," replied Carlos. "What are Rafael and Sofia up to today?" Carlos asked. Rafael was Carlos' oldest child. A sophomore in high school, Rafael had been struggling to engage fully in his classes over the past year. He seemed to prefer spending time playing video games over anything else. On top of that, he had recently turned 16 and been fortunate enough to have his grandparents gift him their old car. And yet, he didn't seem particularly motivated to get his license, so the car sat in the corner of Carlos' driveway, collecting dust, leaves, and the occasional drips of sap from the trees above.

Sofia was Carlos' middle child. She had just turned 14 and was in eighth grade. She would be graduating middle school this year and would be joining her brother in high school next year. And while Sofia seemed more motivated with classes than Carlos, she seemed to require a lot more of Marisol's time than either Rafael or Jose seemed to need. It seemed like Marisol and Sofia had a standing three hour block every evening where they worked on Sofia's school work together.

Marisol thought for a moment before responding, "If I was to guess, Sofia is likely going to spend some time working on a project for school that we've been tackling this week. As for Rafael, I would prefer he either spend time doing some schoolwork or actually preparing for his driver's test in a few weeks. That said, my guess is that as soon as we walk out the door, he is going to go straight to video games."

After a quick and chaotic breakfast with the family, Carlos, Marisol, and Jose were off to the baseball field. Their departure was not near as smooth as they had hoped. Jose had to be told to get ready to go to the game no less than four times. At 9:20 a.m. they arrived at the baseball field, a full 20 minutes late. Marisol popped the trunk and after a few tugs, Jose had his baseball gear over his shoulder and was running toward his team as they were warming up on the field.

The game started at 10:00 a.m. Carlos noticed that as the team took the field, Jose was sitting on the bench. The coach had a rule that if you were late to practice, you would start the game on the bench. As Carlos watched Jose fiddling with a baseball, he noticed that Jose was paying less attention to the game and more to the baseball he was twirling in his hands.

Carlos was about to share his observation with Marisol when another couple plopped down on the bleachers next to them. Carlos and Marisol had known Bill and Sandra since Jose had started playing baseball. Their son, Anthony, had been playing baseball on Jose's team for as long as they could remember. Unlike Jose, Anthony was not laid back. He was a competitive kid, but his competitiveness wasn't reserved for just the opposing team. Anthony was just as likely to knock down a teammate to get to a ball as he would be to knock down an opposing player on his way to second base. Anthony was all about Anthony.

"Hey, you two!" said Sandra cheerfully. "Carlos, what a treat it is to see you. I think it has been almost a year since we saw you on a Saturday." Bill gave a little snicker at Sandra's comment. Carlos feigned a smile, but frankly, he didn't appreciate the dig.

Sandra continued, "Is Jose trying out for the new baseball travel team? Anthony already did a try-out, and the coach says that he just has to have him on the team. You should really think about it. It would be a one-way ticket to a college scholarship."

At that moment, Anthony came over to the fence near the bleachers and began barking at his parents, "Hey Bill...Bill! I need your sunglasses."

Bill looked over at Anthony and just laughed. "What we wouldn't do for our kids," he said to the other adults as he guided his folded sunglasses through the chain link fence to his son.

The game was somewhat anticlimactic. Jose's team lost. He got two at bats and struck out twice. The only interesting events involved Anthony. In the middle of the third inning, Anthony returned the peanut butter sandwich his mom had handed him and said it tasted "horrible." In the fifth inning, Anthony engaged in a heated argument with the head umpire resulting in a warning to the entire team regarding unsportsmanlike conduct.

On the car ride home, Carlos was bothered. The events of the entire morning left him unsettled, but Carlos wasn't quite sure why. And then it hit him. This was an Author vs. Editor issue. He didn't recognize it at first since it wasn't in the workplace. What was so striking about the dynamic between Anthony and his parents was the brazen attitude and sense of hubris Anthony seemed to wield over his parents. He was squarely sitting in the Editor seat, and not in a healthy way. The irony was that Bill and Sandra put Anthony there and seemed to like their arrangement. They were catering to Anthony and taking ownership and initiative over all of Anthony's activities including his apparent happiness. They were Authoring while Anthony was Editing. The result was not pretty.

And then there was Jose. In many ways, Carlos and Marisol were doing something similar toward Jose. Jose had not once demonstrated any ownership, initiative, or critical thinking regarding his baseball activities. He was not Authoring anything. He seemed to just go along with whatever was recommended. It was as if Jose was sitting in the Editor role, but in a more passive way. At that moment, Carlos realized it was time to switch the seats.

"Jose, I have a question for you," Carlos said, from the front seat. "This is your tenth season playing baseball. You've done this long enough to decide on your own if you want to continue to invest the time and energy to continue playing or if you would like to try something new. Think about it and let's talk about it this weekend. Do you want to continue playing baseball after this season or would you like to try something new?"

Jose didn't say anything, but Carlos knew he heard it. Carlos also knew from his own experience of "switching seats" with his team, that it will take some getting used to for Jose.

When they got home, Jose dropped off his baseball stuff in the garage and ran upstairs to take a shower. Carlos decided to test Marisol's theory on how Rafael was going to use his time while they were gone. Sure enough, when Carlos went down to the basement, there was Rafael, hunched over, staring at the television screen in deep concentration as he rapidly maneuvered the video game controller in his hand. At this point, Carlos was a man on an Author vs. Editor mission. Rafael needed to take ownership, display initiative, and show some critical thinking not only with his schoolwork, but also with the parked car in Carlos' driveway that was collecting dust.

"Rafael, have you had lunch yet?" Asked Carlos. After a long pause with no response from Rafael, Carlos cleared his throat and a little more loudly repeated the question. This time, he got a mumbled response of "not yet." Keeping his growing annoyance in check, Carlos said, "Great. When you finish that level, come upstairs and lets you and I have lunch together. There are a few things I want to ask you."

About ten minutes later Rafael groggily came into the kitchen. Carlos had made them both sandwiches and had placed them on two table settings on the kitchen table. Instinctively, Rafael sat down and began to eat.

Carlos started the conversation, "So, how is school going this year?"

Rafael responded between bites, "Fine."

"Huh, well that is interesting. From what I understand from your mother and from some of the teachers, you don't seem particularly engaged or motivated," responded Carlos. He paused but didn't get much of a reaction from Rafael.

After taking a bite of his own sandwich, Carlos continued. "Rafael, from my perspective this is a broader theme for you. Not only do you not seem engaged in school, but you also haven't put forth much effort to get your driver's license, let alone get a job. This needs to change. Here's my question for you: What is holding you back?" Carlos looked over at his son and waited for a response.

After a few more bites, Rafael responded, "I don't know. I guess I just figured you and mom would take care of it for me or at least push me like you always have. Frankly, it is all a little overwhelming."

Carlos gave Rafael a warm smile. "I know it is a lot. And you are right, it can feel very overwhelming. I think in an effort to help you along the way, your mother and I have done you a disservice. We have taken ownership of things in your life, that frankly, are not ours to own. Here's what I propose we do. I want you to think about your goals for this year and I want you to put them down on paper and bring them back to me to discuss tomorrow night after dinner. I want you to specifically answer the following questions for me." With that, Carlos pulled out a piece of paper of his own and passed it over to Rafael. It had the following on it:

> *Our Expectations of You: Ownership, Initiative, and Critical Thinking*
>
> *1) What are your goals for school? What would you like to get accomplished and what are the expectations that you have for yourself? (Note: We don't care what grades you get. What we do care about is that you put forth your best effort, you stretch yourself, and you are proud of the effort that you put in.)*
>
> *2) When would you like to get your driver's license? What do you need to do to be able to achieve that goal?*
>
> *3) When would you like to get a part-time job? What type of jobs interest you the most? What do you need to do to inquire about possible openings?*

One by one, Carlos walked Rafael through the questions. He spent extra time emphasizing that what he and Marisol cared about the most was that Rafael took ownership and initiative with each one and put forth his very best effort. This was not about perfection or about meeting Carlos and Marisol's expectations. It was about meeting Rafael's own expectations of himself. Carlos ended the conversation confirming that Rafael understood what he was asking him to do and that his expectation for the conversation tomorrow evening wasn't that Rafael would have a perfect plan. Rather, Rafael would put forth his best effort in answering the questions above and would bring something for him and Carlos to discuss together. The conversation ended with Carlos giving Rafael a big hug.

When Carlos found Marisol to update her on the conversation he had with Rafael, she appeared upset.

"What's wrong?" Asked Carlos.

"It's Sofia," said Marisol. "I just left her room, and she was crying. While we were at the game, she began working on the school project that I was helping her with this week, and she got herself overwhelmed and worked up. She has decided that her teacher for this class doesn't like her, and she wants me to talk to the teacher for her on Monday."

Carlos could see that Marisol was frustrated. He could also sense that Marisol had become personally invested in Sofia's school work, and it was beginning to take a toll on her. "What are you going to do?" Carlos gently asked.

"Well, I guess I need to set up a meeting with the teacher on Monday and get this resolved," replied Marisol.

"You could do that," responded Carlos. "But at what point would you expect her to take on these conversations herself? I'm just concerned that we might inadvertently send the wrong message to Sofia."

Marisol had a puzzled look on her face. "What do you mean? What wrong message would we be sending to Sofia if I talk to the teacher for her?" Marisol asked.

Carlos looked at Marisol and firmly said, "We would be telling Sofia that she is not enough. That she cannot handle these types of conversations herself. That she needs her parents to do it for her. And if she believes that, in what other parts of her life could she start believing that she isn't enough and she needs us to do it for her."

Carlos paused briefly and then continued, "So let me ask you a question. When you were Sofia's age, how did you handle any issues with a teacher?"

Marisol thought for a moment and responded, "Well, it was all up to me. Neither of my parents spoke any English and they were too busy with work and establishing our life in this country. I handled all of those conversations myself."

With a gentle smile on his face, Carlos continued, "And how did that work for you?"

Marisol nodded her head in understanding, "I see where you are going with this. It gave me the confidence to have these conversations by myself, and it helped me to take charge of my academics and more things in life."

"Let's go for a walk around the neighborhood," said Carlos. I want to share with you a conversation I had with Rafael today. I think you'll find it...interesting."

After a few laps around the neighborhood, Carlos and Marisol walked down the driveway toward their house. Marisol tried to sum up everything she was processing, "After all of our conversations about 'Author versus Editor,' it never occurred to me that the same principles could be applied at home. I feel so incredibly foolish. In an effort to help our kids, I realize now that I've been sitting in the Author seat way too much."

Carlos was not going to let Marisol blame herself. He quickly responded, "Don't beat yourself up. First, it isn't all on you. We've both been sitting in the Author seat with each of them. Second, it's not like you can expect a kindergartner to Author. It just so happens that our kids are at ages where we can start to shift them into the Author seat on certain things. We just need to be intentional to put them in the right seats at the right times."

Later that afternoon, Marisol had a long conversation with Sofia. Marisol started the conversation by telling Sofia how proud of her she was, and that she was confident that Sofia could handle the conversation with her teacher on Monday. Marisol even shared several stories of conversations she had with her teachers when she was Sofia's age and how those boosted her confidence. Marisol also let Sofia know that she was going to be easing off of their nightly schoolwork sessions. "When you are in high school, you can't expect your mom to be helping you with your homework every night. You need to own your own academics," Marisol told Sofia.

When Sunday rolled around, as promised, Carlos met with Rafael after dinner. As Carlos expected, Rafael had some answers to Carlos' questions, but in other areas Rafael was vague. Carlos was pleasantly surprised that Rafael had actually put his answers down in writing.

Over the next hour, Carlos and Rafael discussed Rafael's answers. While not all of Rafael's answers were realistic, Carlos opted to focus on the progress that was made. Carlos ended the conversation by telling Rafael how proud he was of him and gave him another big hug. Carlos ended the conversation by saying, "You've got this, Raf. I know you do. That said, let me and your mom know how we can help you. You've got to take the lead though. For example, we won't be pushing you to drive each week. You'll need to let us know when you want to practice and ask us. That's going to be on you."

As Sunday evening wound down, Carlos went to say goodnight to Jose. As he was tucking Jose into bed, Jose started the conversation, "Dad, I've been thinking about what you said. While I have enjoyed playing baseball, I want to try something different. I don't think I want to play baseball again next season."

Carlos was proud of Jose taking ownership like he had asked, but what surprised Carlos was his own feeling of sadness.

Jose had been playing baseball a long time, and deep down, Carlos really liked watching Jose play. In that moment, there was a part of

Carlos that wanted to convince Jose to give it another try, but he knew that would defeat the entire purpose of the conversation.

"Jose, I'm really proud of you for your decision. What do you think you might want to try instead?" Asked Carlos.

"Well, a few of my friends are in a theater and dance class. It sounds kind of cool. I'd like to try it," replied Jose. And for the next thirty minutes Carlos asked Jose questions about the theater class and an animated Jose went on and on about how fun it sounded.

As Carlos and Marisol were getting ready for bed later that evening, they reflected on the events of the weekend. They were realistic. These were not going to be the only conversations they were going to have with their kids. There was going to be resistance. There were going to be missteps. There were going to be tears. But, in the end, Carlos and Marisol knew they were headed on the right path if they wanted their kids to be Authors in the world.

They turned off their bedroom light and prepared to go to sleep knowing they were going to have some very eventful weeks ahead of them.

Making the Shift from Author to Editor as a Parent

As parents, we all have one overarching goal and purpose: to launch fully formed adults who will make a positive contribution into the world. And yet, how many times have you seen parents inadvertently put their own interests in front of that goal. Consider the following all-too-common parenting missteps:

- The parent that prefers being a friend with their child.
- The parent that likes the feeling of being the "hero/rescuer" and jumps in and solves (or pays for) any problem their child may have (regardless of age).
- The parent that overly controls their child's weekly calendar of activities and micromanages their academics.
- The parent that does their child's laundry, makes their lunch, cleans their room, etc... well into college.

The list could go on. If we look closely at the list above, you can see that each parenting behavior is an Authoring behavior, when an Editing behavior would be more appropriate. And like managers, there are rationalizations for each of these behaviors. Consider the following rationalizations for each behavior listed above as well as the corresponding costs:

- The parent that prefers being a friend with their child.
  - Rationalization: "I don't want them to feel alone. After all, who would be a better unconditional friend than me?"
  - Cost: Unclear decision-making rights and "chain-of-command." In these situations, everything is fine until the parent shifts from a lateral relationship (friend) to a vertical relationship (I'm the boss, here). Not only does it create anger and frustration from the child, but it can also result in heightened levels of anxiety. ("If my mom/dad isn't in charge here, then who is? Me???")

- The parent that likes the feeling of being the "hero/rescuer" and jumps in and solves (or pays for) any problem their child may have (regardless of age).

    - o <u>Rationalization</u>: "I don't want them to have to worry about those problems or issues. I've solved them a million times and it would be easy for me. This way, they can focus on other things."
    - o <u>Cost</u>: Stunted development and a co-dependent relationship. The message that this behavior signals to the child is that "you are not enough. You need me to solve your problems." Overtime, this almost always results in heightened anxiety and fear in a young adult that carries into their adult years.

- The parent that overly controls their child's weekly calendar of activities and micromanages their academics.

    - o <u>Rationalization</u>: "I want them to have all the best opportunities to get into the very best colleges and universities. Harvard, here we come."
    - o <u>Cost</u>: This results in an expectation that others in the "parent" role (Ex: professors, volunteer coordinators, managers, etc...) will do the same thing for them. It results in discomfort with ambiguity and resentfulness if they do everything that they are told to do, and they don't get the pay-off/result that they were promised (Ex: "What do you mean I didn't get the promotion? I did everything that you told me to do.")

- The parent that does their child's laundry, makes their lunch, cleans their room, etc... well into college.
  - o <u>Rationalization</u>: "I'm just making their life easier. They are so busy as it is, plus it makes me feel like I am doing something positive to help them."
  - o <u>Cost</u>: The expectation that someone else will take care of "basics" in life. (Ex: cleaning up after themselves, basic life planning, paying bills, etc...) At minimum it can result in a lag in basic life skills and unnecessary fires. (Ex: "I forgot to pay my bills last month.") At worst, it can result in an entitled attitude, expecting others to Author their basic life needs so they can Edit. (Ex: "Why did you make that for dinner? I didn't want that.")

How and When Do Parents Need to Shift from Author to Editor?

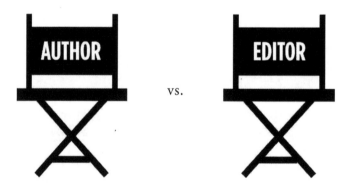

Similar to shifting from Author to Editor as a manager, shifting from Author to Editor as a parent is not as simple as just flipping a light switch. It is more like slowly turning the dial on a dimmer switch. It needs to be a gradual process over time that starts with the basics and ultimately lands with more advanced, complex, and high-stakes activities. How do you know if it is time to shift from Author to Editor as a parent? There are two fundamental signs:

1. **You are exhausted.** Just like Authoring too much at work, if you find you are spending too much of your time doing activities for your child that you were quite capable of doing at their same age and stage of development, that is a sign you need to start shifting seats. Just like at work, once the seats are shifted properly, you'll find you have more time for yourself.
2. **Your child is beginning to act like she or he is in charge.** This is a classic sign that you have been in the Author seat for so long that your child has begun to intuitively assume the Editor seat. However, unlike our ideal Editor, children will corrupt the seat and show up more like demanding critics and pint-sized autocrats. If you find yourself with a demanding critic living under your roof, it is time to shift the seats.

Below is a sample of possibly appropriate Authorship activities that you can shift to your child based on her or his age.

<u>Note</u>: All the below suggested Authorship activities are simply that—suggestions. As a parent, you must use your best judgment given you and your family's particular situation as well as your child's maturity and personality.

<u>*Disclaimer*</u>: Our parenting styles and approaches are very personal and deeply held. In no way am I suggesting that you are not doing your "job"

as a parent if you don't follow the suggestions below. Rather, my goal is to offer you some perspectives on ways to help you achieve your end goal of raising healthy, competent, and confident adults who are capable of approaching life with "ownership, initiative, and critical-thinking." In short, I'm on your team!

Age of Child / Young Adult	Role of Parent (You)	Authorship Expectations of the Child / Young Adult
0–9 Years Old	100% Author / 0% Editor **AUTHOR**	In this early stage of parenting, the parent essentially Authors the child's world from the activities that she or he participates in, to the food on the table. Note: There aren't any "real" Editor rights given to the child in this stage. In other words, if the child doesn't like what is for dinner, they do not technically have the power to change that. However, as the parent you can choose to honor her or his opinion and make changes. Just be careful that you don't inadvertently give them permission to have Editor rights over you. As I regularly told my kids growing up: "Decision makers pay." If they aren't paying for dinner, they do not have decision-making rights. An opinion, sure. A position of power in the household is a dangerous thing to give to a five year-old. And yet, how many parents make this misstep?

Age of Child / Young Adult	Role of Parent (You)	Authorship Expectations of the Child / Young Adult
10–12 Years Old	90% Author / 10% Editor	In these "tween" years, Authorship could include any of the following: • Deciding what extracurricular activities that the child still wants to participate in and what else she or he may want to explore • Cleaning their room without being asked • Making her or his own lunch every day before school Note: In the examples above, the parent has Editor rights to evaluate the child's work product / decisions and adjust/coach accordingly. (Ex: "While I see why you might want to only pack yogurt for lunch, let's talk about other items that you need to include.")

Age of Child / Young Adult	Role of Parent (You)	Authorship Expectations of the Child / Young Adult
13–15 Years Old	70% Author / 30% Editor	In these early teen years, Authorship could include any of the following (in addition to the items in prior stages): • Responsible for getting and completing her or his schoolwork (assignments, studying for tests, etc...) without assistance or direction from a parent • Doing her or his own laundry from start to finish (Ex: sorting, proper washer and dryer settings, folding and putting the clothes away) • The ability (and encouragement) to have conversations with teachers and other authority figures to discuss needs, concerns, and questions without a parent present (or interceding) Note: As in the prior examples, in the examples above the parent has Editor rights to evaluate the child's work product / decisions and adjust/coach accordingly.

Age of Child / Young Adult	Role of Parent (You)	Authorship Expectations of the Child / Young Adult
16–18 Years Old	50% Author / 50% Editor	In these mid-to-late teen years, Authorship could include any of the following (in addition to the items in prior stages): • Initiative to find an entry level job in order to earn money for leisure / non-necessities (Note: volunteer activities should not be confused with employment. Volunteers have Editing power because they are "paying" with their time and not getting "paid" to be there.) • Owning one's overall academics including selecting her/his classes as well as her/his path after graduation (Ex: applying to college, joining the armed forces, starting a business, etc...) • Responsible for identifying the necessary steps to acquiring a driver's license and owning the process (Ex: They are asking parents for time to practice and not the other way around.) Note: As in the prior examples, in the examples above the parent has Editor rights to evaluate the young adult's work product / decisions and adjust/coach accordingly.

Age of Child / Young Adult	Role of Parent (You)	Authorship Expectations of the Child / Young Adult
19–23 Years Old	30% Author / 70% Editor	In these late teen and young adult years, Authorship could include any of the following (in addition to the items in prior stages): • Day-to-day management of life tasks (Ex: getting to appointments/class, meals, hygiene, laundry, etc...) • Greater responsibility over life "maintenance" (Ex: going to the dentist, getting the oil changed in one's car, getting one's phone repaired, etc...) • Responsible for owning "performance" (Ex: passing classes, getting to work on time, etc...) • Responsible for defining one's career next step (Ex: internship and job search post college, defining one's career goals over the next 1–3 years, etc...) Note: As in the prior examples, in the examples above the parent has Editor rights to evaluate the young adult's work product / decisions and adjust/coach accordingly.

Age of Child / Young Adult	Role of Parent (You)	Authorship Expectations of the Child / Young Adult
24–27 Years Old	0% Author / 0% Editor	In these early adult years, Authorship could include any of the following (in addition to the items in prior stages): • Paying all of one's living expenses • Keeping a balanced budget and not going into unintentional debt • Defining the types of relationships that one is looking for in life (personally and professionally) • Owning and defining one's longer-term career path Note: If done properly, the parent should have NEITHER Author rights NOR Editor rights at this point. Congratulations, you would have launched a fully formed adult into the world.

Warnings for Parents Shifting from Author to Editor at Home

Whether we are managers or parents, shifting from Author to Editor has its challenges. While I have addressed many of the challenges and obstacles related to this shift in prior chapters, I want to highlight a few particularly "emotional" obstacles to be on the lookout for as you attempt to make the shift. Afterall, there are few things as emotional as parenting. Consider the following:

>**Trap #1: Too much personal "ownership" leading to poor boundaries.** Just like with managers not wanting to let go of activities that they were once directly responsible for, a similar trap can happen with parents. There can be a tendency to "feel" like you are the one making everything happen, and if you stop pushing, orchestrating, and driving, nothing will happen. In this trap, the parent becomes emotionally invested in owning the process and the lines become blurred on whether this is the child's activity or the parent's activity.
>
>Perhaps nothing captures this sentiment better than a comment that a parent made to me a few years ago when they were helping their child prepare for an AP Calculus exam. After I asked them how their weekend was, they responded with the following, "We stayed up all night studying for the AP Calculus exam. There were some questions that we didn't anticipate, but we think we did pretty well." We? Really? Talk about poor boundaries.
>
>**Trap #2: Be wary of emotional "sunk costs."** If you haven't heard of the term "sunk costs" before, it is often used in Managerial

Accounting to refer to when a manager continues to invest in a failing initiative because they are already so heavily invested that they don't want to simply walk away. (Ex: I know we are over budget by $2M, but with another $1M, I know we can get the project completed.)

This rears its ugly head when we make the shift from Author to Editor, and our child announces that she or he no longer wants to play piano, go to karate, swim competitively, play baseball, etc. The logical response is, "I hear you. Let's discuss your rationale and what you would like to do alternatively." But in this case, we begin to imagine all of those Saturdays that they (and we) invested in recitals, tournaments, and meets. We imagine all the progress they made from five years old to 12 years old and we just can't bear to walk away. Why? Because the thought of walking away feels akin to letting something we cherish die. We begin to grieve. We don't like the feeling, so we push on the child to "give it one more try."

Sadly, they agree. From personal experience, I have felt the pain and sadness of this trap. I just have to remind myself that it isn't about me.

Trap #3: To Author is to be vulnerable and with Authoring comes missteps and disappointment. When a parent makes the shift into the Editor seat and allows their child to Author, there will be mistakes. There will be disappointments. There will be tears. From ruined laundry to failed assignments at school because the directions weren't properly followed, there will inevitably be situations in which our child will experience disappointment, pain, and tears streaming down their cheeks. And when the tears come, we as parents, feel that pain just as profoundly as they do (and in some cases, I could make the argument that we feel it worse as it triggers some of our own past experiences). No one likes this feeling, let alone seeing their child suffer the same pain that we once felt so deeply.

As a result, there is a strong temptation for the parent to jump in and Author a solution to make the pain go away. When we do that, the pain, in fact, does immediately go away. And our child thanks us. But the long-term damage is done. Our child never develops the resilience necessary to know how to get back up and take ownership, show initiative, and display critical thinking.

When we routinely swoop in and rescue our children, we stunt their growth and prevent them from developing agency in life. They learn that they are not enough.

So, parents, as painful as it may be for everyone involved, let the tears fall and the sadness persist until both have run their respective courses. Only then will your kiddo develop the strength and resilience to try again and learn that failure won't break them.

A Word of Encouragement

Shifting from being an Author to an Editor is difficult regardless of whether we are a senior manager or a parent of a 13-year-old. That said, I hope this chapter illuminated several other aspects of this critical shift. In short, if we want others to take ownership, show initiative, and display critical thinking, we have to do the hard work. The good news is that when we start this process with one member of our family (or team), we are changing the culture, and pretty soon, by the time we get to the third child (or third new hire), we find they already "get it."

Making this shift at home is hard emotional work.

And you know what?

It is worth every bit of the effort.

Reflection Questions for You from Chapter 6

- Can you identify with any of the four parenting missteps (behaviors, rationalizations, and costs) identified above? If so, what have those missteps been costing you and your child?
- Are you ready to begin making the shift from Author to Editor at home? If so, why are you ready now?
- Based on the age of your child/children, in what ways have you been effectively shifting into an Editor mode (requiring them to make their own lunch for school, for example)? In what ways could you improve?
- Have you experienced any of the three emotional traps when moving from Author to Editor at home? If so, how could you more intentionally protect yourself from falling into those traps in the future?
- If you still have children at home, what is your longer-term plan (or your plan with your partner) to effectively move your children from the Editor seat into the Author seat in order to get them ready for adulthood?

CHAPTER 7

Knowing When and How to Author as a Leader

Present Day…

IT HAD BEEN nearly a month since Carlos shared his own story as a struggling 38-year-old director some twenty years ago with his mentee, David Springer, and how the concept Author vs. Editor helped him reset his life. Since that initial meeting with David, they had been meeting almost weekly and Carlos was beginning to see the progress from David that he had hoped. Carlos was anxious to get an update from the rest of his senior team on how Operation: Author vs. Editor was going across the company.

Unfortunately, he was still stuck on the phone with Ken Banfield, a member of the board of directors, for a little over an hour. While this call with Ken was important (there was a board meeting in a month), Ken had gotten on one of his soapboxes, and they were already a few minutes over on their scheduled time with no sign of Ken running out of steam anytime soon. Carlos gently interrupted Ken as he was extolling on the virtues of supply chain diversification. "Ken, I really appreciate your time today. Unfortunately, I have a very critical meeting with my senior team that I need to attend to. Would you like me to call you later today so we can continue our conversation?"

After realizing that he had lost track of time, Ken politely responded, "No Carlos. My apologies. You know me... sometimes I get carried away. Overall, I feel very confident in the direction that you would like to take the next board conversation. No need for us to have an additional call. I look forward to seeing you at the meeting next month."

With that Carlos ended the call, and made his way to his door. Waiting outside of his office was Cynthia, his executive assistant. She was standing as poised as usual, holding a folder in her outstretched hands labeled "Operation: Author vs. Editor." As she handed Carlos the envelope, they both began striding toward the Board room. As Cynthia matched Carlos' pace effortlessly, she updated him on the contents of the envelope.

"Everyone has submitted their meeting reports as well as the meeting logs of their direct reports. The good news is that all of the meetings are going as planned. The not-so-good news is that the problem is as deep and as pervasive as you had feared." Cynthia paused for a reaction.

Carlos simply nodded his head in understanding. After a few moments, he replied to Cynthia, "Is there anything else that I need to be aware of before the meeting?"

"No, there aren't any other big highlights. On a positive note, I did hear from David Springer, the young man that you've been meeting with as part of Operation: Author vs. Editor. He is seeing some significant progress with his team and for the first time in months, he didn't work at all over the weekend. He said he wanted me to tell you that his wife was very appreciative of all of your help." Cynthia gave Carlos a warm smile. She knew that Carlos cared as much about the personal and professional lives of everyone in the company as much as he did about overall company performance.

Carlos opened the doors to the conference room and he and Cynthia made their way to their seats at the furthest end of the table.

"My apologies for being a few minutes late," Carlos stated. "That said, I've been very much looking forward to this meeting. I'd like to spend the first half of the meeting getting updates from each of you regarding your first few rounds of 'Author vs. Editor' conversations with your direct reports. After that, I want to dig into the role of leaders as 'Authors' for their teams in more detail. We spend so much time avoiding 'Authoring' that it is important that we identify the ways in which we still need to be 'Authoring' with our teams. This conversation will ensure that we are all on the same page as we continue to help our teams make these critical shifts."

After a solid thirty minutes of updates, Carlos heard story after story of leaders throughout the organization sitting in the wrong seats. They were Authoring way too often when they should be Editing, and as a result, burnout was approaching an unsustainable level across the company. To make matters worse, there wasn't growth and development in the way that should be occurring throughout the organization. In other words, the irony was that while leaders were working 65-plus hours a week, they weren't working on the "right" things that would develop them to move to the next level. They were deep in the weeds doing the work of their teams instead of working on tasks that might prepare them for the next level. The good news is that every member of the senior team received positive feedback to the concept of Author vs. Editor and over the course of the first few meetings, progress was beginning to be made.

After reassuring the team that they were on the right path and to keep up the conversations, Carlos reviewed the most common traps with the team to remind them to be vigilant. From the "Hero Trap" to reminding his team that to Author is to be vulnerable, they hit all of the high notes. "The only thing standing in the way of you helping your teams make this shift is you," Carlos emphasized. "If you are focused, disciplined, and intentional, you'll see the majority of your teams make the shifts necessary in just a matter of months." With that closing comment, Carlos began to pivot the conversation.

"We haven't spent much time on when to properly 'Author' as a leader. As a reminder, we need to be sitting in the 'Editor' seat 80% of the time and the 'Author' seat 20% of the time. Specifically, there are two big categories that only we, as leaders, can Author," Carlos paused for a moment to make sure he had everyone's attention as he made his way to the white board in the room. He grabbed a marker and wrote: **1. Strategy/Priorities** on the board.

"The first major item that we need to be 'Authoring' with our teams is *Strategy* and *Priorities*. In my mind, these are two separate things. *Strategy* represents our broader goals, objectives, and overall strategy for the quarter or more broadly, the year. It is important that we are regularly continuing this drumbeat, so our teams don't get distracted by all of the daily noise and fires that emerge in the business."

Carlos had just finished his thought when Angela Bates, his Chief Marketing Officer, interjected. "Carlos, I understand the need to keep our teams focused on the longer-term strategy for the year, but the competing demands of the business that we face every week are overwhelming. How is reminding our teams of our one, or even three-year strategic plan going to help very much?"

Carlos appreciated Angela's question. One of Carlos' favorite traits about Angela was her fearlessness in the senior team meetings and her willingness to ask the tough questions. She was the company's youngest executive and had earned her place at the table as a result of her boldness and willingness to embrace change. Angela had a tough upbringing. She grew up in a poor neighborhood and dysfunctional household. Through sheer will and determination, she put herself through college and had been a rising star ever since she joined the company 15 years ago.

Carlos responded, "Angela, I completely agree. Strategy is important, but we need another term to help us combat the weekly fires that we are always facing. That is why you see the word *Priorities* written on the board. When I use the term *Priorities*, I am talking about *Strategy* with a small 's.' I'm referring to the goals, objectives and strategy for a given *week*. Our teams can easily be overwhelmed by the many urgent demands and competing agendas that are thrown at them. It is critical that we don't get overcome by the tyranny of the urgent. That said, it is our job to 'Author' to our teams weekly the key priorities for that given week."

Carlos paused and looked around the room. He saw his leaders furiously taking notes. He reminded himself that he had a really solid leadership team made up of some exceptional people. He knew that they intuitively got what he was telling them. That said, even the best leaders can be easily distracted by the noise of the business. This was a reminder for them to keep their "eye on the ball," and not get distracted by less critical issues.

"The central task of communicating the weekly priorities to the team is the primary reason that I always make it a point to emphasize the key priorities for each week when we meet as a senior team every Monday. Do any of you have any questions regarding this first point regarding our role as 'Authors' in the business?" Carlos panned the room and he saw heads nodding back and forth that they had no further questions. With that confirmation, Carlos went back to the whiteboard and wrote: **2. Culture** in equally bold black letters.

"Similar to *Strategy and Priorities*, the term *Culture* has two different definitions that we are responsible for Authoring with our teams. First, let's look at *Culture* with a big 'C.' This is our company culture. In many ways, we have done an acceptable job of articulating this and reinforcing this in many of the activities that we do. That said, we can never do too much when it comes to company culture. Just like I attempt to do with my monthly messages to the company, I need your help in reinforcing, restating, and 'Authoring' what those values mean to your teams. Culture only thrives when all of the leaders are on the same page." Carlos had barely ended his thought when Angela jumped in with another question.

"Carlos, my apologies if I'm not following you, but didn't we already do that work? We spent nearly a full week this year articulating our new corporate values. To reinforce those values, we had them included in all company-wide communications and even had them painted on the walls in every meeting room." As she was making her point, Angela motioned to the five words painted above the white board directly behind Carlos.

Angela was right, Carlos thought. They had done a tremendous amount of work already to identify and articulate the values. So, what was he really asking them to do now? At that point, an image popped into Carlos' head.

Carlos began to elaborate, "Angela, you are spot on. We have done a lot of work regarding values this year. But our work is not done. A good way to think about this concept would be to think of culture as an orchestra. An orchestra, by definition, is a collection of disparate people and instruments, just like our company is a collection of different people, different departments, and various functions. The work we did earlier this year when we wrote out the company values was the equivalent of giving everyone the same piece of music to play. But just like with an orchestra, that wouldn't be enough."

Carlos paused to let the point sink in before he continued. "Orchestras need conductors and 'first chairs' of the different instruments. My job as CEO is similar to that of the orchestra conductor. I need to ensure that everyone is hitting the right notes at the right time. That said, if I'm the only one who is on beat and holding the timing of the group, our alignment and collective performance is going to be horrendous. However, if we, as leaders of the business and of our respective functions, are all on the same beat and reinforcing and emphasizing the same notes at the same time, just like different instruments in an orchestra, we will create a beautiful and collective performance."

Carlos looked around to see if his analogy was sticking. He needed to look no further than Cynthia as she was nodding in enthusiastic approval.

Carlos looked at Angela and responded, "Does my way of thinking about culture make sense?"

Angela thought for a moment and said, "Yes, it makes perfect sense. That said, I don't think I thought of it as an on-going activity. I figured we did all the hard work when we identified those five values. I thought our work was done. I realize after this conversation that there is still more work to be done."

After agreeing with Angela, Carlos posed the following to the group: "So, the question for each of you is this: 'Are you doing as much as you can to reinforce our company culture?'" Carlos let a long uncomfortable moment of silence linger after his question, so the point truly set in with his team. Similar to Angela, he knew there was more that could be done by every leader in the room to improve on this critical task.

Carlos continued, "Hopefully, that analogy reminds each of you of the importance of all of our roles in reinforcing company culture. And just like *Strategy*, *Culture* also has a little 'c' as well. This little 'c' represents the culture of your team. Are you doing enough to share your values and expectations with your teams? You may likely find an overlap with the broader values of our company culture and the values that you would like to promote with your team and department. That said, each of your teams and your functions have different goals and objectives. And each of you are different people and different leaders. You will no doubt find that there are some values that you want to emphasize that are unique to your function and your team. That is okay. The key is to identify those values, regularly communicate them, and most importantly, act in accordance with them."

Before Carlos could finish, Martin, the Chief Technology Officer, chimed in, "Carlos, could you provide us with an example of values unique to our teams. I would be curious as to how you might see our team values differ from our company values."

Carlos was slightly taken aback by Martin's question. It wasn't that he was offended, he just didn't have an obvious example. Then the perfect example hit him. "For example, think about the whole 'Author versus Editor' journey that we are on. You may want to particularly emphasize the need for 'Authorship' with your team. In the process, if you inadvertently become a critic rather than a coach, you would be undermining not just the values of Authorship, the values of *Ownership, Initiative,* and *Critical Thinking,* but also any other values that you have been trying to put in place with your team. Culture requires consistent actions and decisions across the board to keep it alive and well. One inconsistent move and trust in the culture is broken." Once again, Carlos paused for emphasis. He needed his leaders to be keeping culture top of mind, particularly if Operation: Author vs. Editor was going to work. And it had to work. There was simply no other way forward for the business.

Carlos moved to a blank space on the whiteboard and wrote the following: ***Homework: Define your list of 3–5 values for <u>your team</u> and send the list to Cynthia by <u>next Monday</u>***.

"Defining your team and your department's unique culture is so important that I want you to spend some time on that task this week. Once you have defined your team's values, the values that you believe are important to your team and department's success, send those to Cynthia no later than next Monday. As you will see on the board, your list must be limited to three to five. Any more than that, and you are simply diluting what really matters. Worse, you will be making it increasingly difficult for your team to remember the values that you are trying to emphasize. The same principle of three to five also applies for your weekly priorities with your team. If you are giving your team more than five priorities to manage in a given week, you will be diluting focus to a point that you'll actually create chaos—the exact thing that we are all trying to prevent."

Carlos moved away from the whiteboard and sat back down in his seat. "In keeping with both the idea of 'Author vs. Editor' and in an effort to reinforce the values of ownership and initiative with this team, I am going to propose a change to our leadership team meetings going forward. Rather than leading our senior team meetings like I have in the past, starting next week, I am going to rotate the ownership of each meeting amongst this team. This will give each of you the opportunity to set the agenda and lead a senior team discussion. Of course, I still plan to attend all of these meetings, but I will play more of an 'Editor' or 'coach' role to help each of you to improve how you lead these types of meetings and discussions going forward. Look for Cynthia to send out the meeting rotation later this afternoon."

After a few more housekeeping items and some brief discussion regarding "to do" items to get accomplished before the next meeting, Carlos adjourned the meeting a full five minutes ahead of schedule.

As everyone was gathering their belongings and exiting the conference room, Martin waited until the room was almost cleared out and approached Carlos. "Carlos, you made a really important reference to the chaotic nature of the business and our need for prioritization. I specifically liked your comment about the tyranny of the urgent. It is my belief that in addition to managing priorities, I think it is equally important that we manage our use of urgency in the business. One of my direct reports, Kate, has a fantastic analogy for urgency that has really helped how we manage urgency in the IT function."

With that, Martin handed Carlos a small miniature bottle of hot sauce. "We use these throughout our department, and it really has made a difference. During our next one-on-one this week, I'll fill you in on the idea." With that, Martin thanked Carlos for the meeting and made his way out of the room.

Carlos turned the small bottle of hot sauce in his hands and wondered where the conversation might go with Martin. And yet, seeing Martin's enthusiasm and the sense of 'Authorship' that was coming from him and his team, put a bright smile on Carlos' face.

Leaders Need to Author 20% of the Time

Many years ago, I had the pleasure to work with an aerospace engineering company. This company literally made and tested rockets. So, it was one of the rare occasions when my dad jokes could actually find a place in the workplace. You see, my task was to help this firm articulate its already amazing culture. Where's the dad joke you may say? Well, in most cases culture isn't rocket science, but in this case, it absolutely was. (As you are reading this, somewhere in the world one of my children is rolling her or his eyes.)

The leader of the business was an impressive young CEO. His mother had started the business as one of the first female aerospace Ph.D.'s and when she came close to retirement age, she handed the business to my client. My client is a smart guy in his own right (Ph.D. in biology), but he was no rocket scientist. That said, he intuitively knew culture. Through his leadership, his company was winning contract after contract with NASA and the U.S. Department of Defense. My job was to help them understand exactly what they were doing that was creating such a winning culture. After I finished my work with the company and delivered the findings in a report to my client, he made the decision to "turn up the volume" on the culture that he had established and really double down on values that made their business so great.

And then something strange began to happen.

My client called me about three months after he started his initiative to double down on culture with some unexpected news. People were leaving. He was more than a little concerned at this surprising turn of events. They had never experienced much turnover in the history of the business up to that point. I, frankly, wasn't quite sure what to do. So, I told him to keep watching this unexpected trend and give me a call in about a month.

A month later, my client called me, as promised. However, his tone was quite different on this call. He relayed to me that yes, people had left the business. But after the dust settled, and he and his team began to look more closely at the individuals that had left, they realized that all of the exits were due to cultural mismatches. So, in other words, these folks were no longer good fits for the business. They were the "right people" to exit at that time. And then he shared with me this analogy:

> "It was like our company was similar to the fish tank you see at a dentist's office. We were all the fish in the tank swimming about. Without articulating and reinforcing the culture of the business, the water in the fish tank was murky and cloudy. We couldn't see other fish in the tank, and they couldn't see us." He continued:

> *"Once we started to intentionally share, reinforce, and act on our stated values, it was like we cleaned the water. Just like the water, our culture became crystal clear."*

My client then extended the metaphor a bit further, concluding: "And then, we could see the fish that were hanging out at the bottom of the fish tank and weren't swimming in the school with the rest of us. And they could see us. It became painfully apparent to those fish that they either needed to get in the school with the rest of the fish or find another tank. And some of them opted to find another tank."

I love that story as a way to establish the importance of setting, emphasizing, and reinforcing culture. And as a leader, it is one of those activities that is not only critical, but is also one of the few activities that only we as leaders can Author.

When and How to Author as a Leader

Up until now, nearly every chapter of this book has been dedicated to the importance of leaders sitting in the Editor seat. And given that should represent 80% of your time, the emphasis makes complete sense. However, there is still that lingering 20% that we need to address. It is in this 20% of the time that you should be Authoring with your team. As this chapter outlines, there are two primary activities that you should be Authoring:

1) Communicate Your Strategy/Priorities. This category is critical for keeping your team focused. It is about defining the discrete goals and objectives for the team in a given time frame. These can be lumped into two critical categories:

    a. <u>Strategy with a Big "S"</u> — These are the items that are the critical goals and priorities for the year. It has been my experience that the most effective organizations execute off of a list of no more than three to five annual priorities. Examples might be any of the following:

        i. "Grow top-line revenue by 10%"
        ii. "Increase overall profitability by 15%"
        iii. "Decrease supply chain costs by 13%"
        iv. "Increase market share by 5%"
        v. "Increase our gross admissions numbers by 10% (University)"

b. <u>Strategy with a Little "s"</u> — These are the weekly priorities for the business or the team. Similar to the "Big Strategy," the most effective teams execute off of three to five weekly priorities that are set by the leader. These weekly priorities are arguably more important than the longer-term priorities due to the noise and competing demands that most organizations and teams face on a weekly basis. In my previous book, *<u>The Hot Sauce Principle: How to Live and Lead in a World Where Everything Is Urgent All of the Time</u>*, there is tremendous emphasis placed on leaders ensuring that they aren't making everything urgent. Setting a discrete list of priorities each week and protecting one's team from all of the "noise" in the business, is one of the antidotes. Examples might be any of the following:

  i. "Ensure that project Phoenix is running on schedule"
  ii. "Get out the month-end financials by Friday"
  iii. "Close the deal with XYZ company by Q2"
  iv. "Respond to any customer requests or issues within 24 hours"
  v. "Grade all final exams and submit final grades by end of the week (School)"

2) Articulate and Reinforce Your Culture. Like *Strategy/Priorities*, *Culture* has two components, a "Big C" and a "Little C." Also like *Strategy/Priorities*, the most effective cultures, whether they are organizational culture or team culture, operate off of a list of three to five values. Where there is a difference is that Culture is about the "how" of the work, while *Strategy/Priorities* is about the "what" and the "when" of the work.

I had a culture expert on my podcast a few years ago. During the conversation, we stumbled on this analogy. Culture is a lot like the lenses that we look through. I wear glasses and have worn glasses since I was in fourth grade. Every year, I'm supposed to go to the optometrist to get my eyes checked. That said, in reality, I go about every three years. Culture is the same way. It is the set of lenses that you are giving everyone in your organization or team to look through. And just like our eyes, what we need to be paying attention to from a cultural perspective can change as our industries change, customers change and the competitive landscape changes.

a. <u>Culture with a "Big C"</u> — This is our organizational culture. These are the three to five values that are critical for the organization to be successful in carrying out its strategy today. It is our job to Author these for our organization, so they not only know "how" they need to be operating, but also who they need to be selecting and deselecting based on the culture.

<u>An Example of Using Values to Select the Right Cultural Fit</u>

Some years ago, I was working with a client organization that was highly technical. They would typically look to hire experts in their respective field that came with many advanced degrees and credentials. In addition to their technical expertise and corresponding values related to precision, quality, and skill, one of their unique corporate values was "Humility." This firm had a very creative way to evaluate candidates on this particular value.

The interview process took a full, jam-packed day. They would fly in candidates for interviews and would send a driver to meet them at the airport to take them to the office. Once at the office, candidates would start their journey with the receptionist and throughout the day, they would be put through a series of interviews with senior leaders as well as other technical experts in the firm. Sometimes the interviews were one on one and sometimes there were full "teams" interviewing these candidates.

After the grueling day, the driver would take the candidate back to the airport. What the candidate didn't know during this entire process was that the decision was actually being made by only one of the individuals that the candidate had met during the day. And that decision maker, the person ultimately deciding whether or not the candidate was going to join the team, was the driver.

You see, they already knew the candidates that they were selecting had all of the expertise necessary given their degrees and designations. What they didn't know is how they treated people when the candidate thought no one was looking. Hence, it was the driver who ultimately determined culture fit.

b. <u>Culture with a "Little c"</u> — This is all about Authoring your team culture. First, it is important to note that every leader is setting a culture with their team. The best leaders clearly articulate their culture. The less-than-best leaders practice what I call "Las Vegas Management." They have their values and are rewarding and punishing their team based on those values. They just aren't telling anyone what those values are. They are letting others guess and gamble. When they guess right, they win. And when they guess wrong, they lose. The best leaders Author their list of three to five values for their team and they regularly communicate those to their team. Note: Your team values DO NOT have to be the mirror image of your organization's values. The values necessary to have a high performing Marketing Department might not be the same values necessary to have a high performing Finance Department. You just want to ensure that the values you do select are close relatives to the broader organization.

An Example of Articulating Your Team Values

I was recently working with a senior leader who took over a business with a long history of a "command and control" culture. He desperately wanted to change that. As he shared with his direct reports, as a natural problem solver, it was his natural tendency to jump in and solve problems. But if he did that, he would be simply reinforcing the old culture. (Team members would come to him and ask him to tell them what to do. He would perpetually be in the Author seat.)

He had recently gone to a doctor's appointment with his teenage son. As the conversation turned to parenting, the doctor told my client that if he always solved problems for his son, his son would never develop the neural wiring that comes from solving problems on one's own.

My client later relayed that story to his team and said rather than jumping in and solving all of the problems presented to him from his team (and limiting their abilities to think critically), he was going to change the culture by responding with, **"What do you think we should do?"** That didn't mean he would always agree, but it was designed to get everyone in the business thinking about solutions, not just him.

In addition to the critical Author seats outlined above, there are two other occasions when Authoring is appropriate. Consider the following:

- **Onboarding a New Team Member.** When we onboard a new team member, not only would it be unfair to require them to genuinely Author from "Day One," it is also important that we walk alongside them to educate them on the culture of the business. Consider this a "co-Authoring" assignment that should last no more than six months.
- **Extreme Or Unusual Emergencies.** I want to make an important distinction here. "Every day" emergencies do not count as Authoring situations. Only those situations that require your unique expertise or your vast knowledge, and in both cases, when team members possess neither, that you should fully engage.

Let me share an example of how to do this the "right way." Several months ago, I was coaching a plant manager. After celebrating the wins of his team on a late afternoon, he was about to leave when a critical machine in the plant broke down. As an engineer by training, in the past, this manager would have jumped in to solve the problem. This time, however, he let his team Author the solution. He told them that he trusted them, and he went home. By the next morning, the machinery had been repaired in record time.

Warnings for Leaders When They Are Authoring for Their Teams

Trap #1: Being so busy doing the work that you don't Author priorities or culture for your team. Perhaps the most common trap, it is easy for leaders to become so busy that they don't set aside the time to communicate priorities or culture for their teams. If we don't communicate priorities or culture for our team, rather than having a world-class orchestra, we will end up with our team performing much like a sixth-grade band class during the first few weeks of school. Not music to anyone's ears.

Trap #2: We give our team more than five priorities in a given week to accomplish. If you are interested in creating a workplace concoction of massive chaos and confusion complete with a heaping spoonful of anxiety, give your teams a double-digit list of "priorities" to accomplish in a given week. We've all heard the adage, "If everything is a priority, then nothing is a priority." This trap reminds me of one of the mantras I would share with my classes when we were discussing the topic of leadership communication. I would preach to the class that when we communicate at work, whether that is an e-mail, a conversation, or a given presentation, we are either adding value or diluting from existing value. Communicating our priorities definitely applies to this mantra. Too many priorities will dilute what really matters.

Trap #3: We "co-Author" the culture with our team. This trap feels counter intuitive. You are probably saying to yourself, "Brandon, isn't it a good idea to bring my team into this discussion? Afterall,

I want to create buy-in, joint ownership and a sense of unity when we roll out culture." And if that sentiment represents how you feel, you are not wrong. However, there is one critical difference. You are the leader. And as the leader, you have to talk about and model culture. Every. Single. Day. Given your unique role as the leader, or champion of the culture, the values that you come up with must first resonate with you. Then, you can bring in your team re: the fine print. In other words, I want you to define the three to five values that you believe are critical to success and then allow your team to help you "co-Author" the description of those values and what those values look like in action (the behaviors). You still get the benefit of their involvement, and you promote team buy-in while still maintaining the deep connection between you and the values of the culture.

To reinforce my point, I want you to think about the companies, organizations, and teams that you admire the most. Perhaps it is the results that they achieve, or perhaps you admire them more for the way they go about achieving the results that they achieve. Regardless of your criteria, I want you to consider the list. I think you would be hard-pressed in those examples to find a "democratic" approach to identifying the team or organization's values. World class teams and organizations typically have a leader or leaders that have a very strong point of view tied to a particular value or values. That passion and focus helps to spread the value and make it contagious. A steely will and a healthy dose of passion for a value or values is critical with any strong culture. The most powerful values come from a leader's heart, not from a committee.

Trap #4: Culture is treated as a "one and done" activity. How many times have you experienced this scenario: A senior team goes away for a few days to identify (or refresh) the core values of the organization. After several days holing up at a retreat center, they come back excited to announce the "new" values of the organization. With great fanfare, they introduce the new values to the organization. There might even be fancy posters or a big presentation. And then...nothing. Crickets. It's as if there is this underlying notion that, "Hey, we said it once to everyone. That should be enough."

If we take that same idea and apply it to parenting, we realize how ridiculous that belief really is in actual practice. No parent in the history of humankind has ever been able to tell their child to clean their room only once and have it stick from that point forward without any need to bring it up again. There is a greater probability of winning the lottery than delivering a world-class lecture to one of your kiddos and have it be "one and done." Culture, just like parenting, requires reps. You can't do the "reps" one time and expect meaningful results.

And just like "reps" with your workouts, you can overcome this trap by making culture a disciplined routine. Perhaps you talk about and reinforce culture with your team every month. Or better, perhaps you find a way to share a culture tie-in weekly during your team meetings. Regardless, communicating and reinforcing culture needs to be a disciplined practice.

There you have it. A chapter solely dedicated to when and how you should be Authoring with your team. And while this isn't rocket science (Eddie's company aside), just like your physical health, it requires discipline and consistently. By regularly communicating and reinforcing the critical priorities and desired culture to your team, you will not only keep the team aligned, but also focused on the right things. And if you ask me, there is no greater gift that you can give your team than that level of clarity.

So, dear leader, Author away!

Reflection Questions for You from Chapter 7

- Are you properly Editing in the other areas (80%) to give yourself enough time to Author only the things that you can Author (20%)?
- Does your team know your broader goals and strategy for the year? Are you regularly communicating it?
- Does your team know their weekly priorities and are you effective at keeping the list of priorities to five or less?
- How could you improve your consistency in your communication of priorities to your team? Consider team meetings, recorded videos, e-mail messages, and your 1:1 conversations with team members as possible avenues to explore.
- Are you regularly and consistently communicating your desired team culture with your team? How could you improve your message? Is it frequency? Do you need to share more stories and examples? Are you recognizing team members that are embodying the culture in the way that you desire?

Chapter 8

How to Maintain an Author vs. Editor Mindset

A FEW WEEKS had passed since Carlos had met with his senior team to discuss their roles as Authors in the business, and Carlos and Cynthia were animatedly discussing Carlos' calendar for the upcoming month.

"Carlos, I just don't know if that is a good idea," Cynthia said as she eyed Carlos across the table.

"But I've always attended the weekly status update meetings with my executive team," Carlos said with a plea in his voice. "And don't let us forget that I was the one who implemented those meetings and was personally leading those meetings for the last three years," Carlos added in an effort to further make his case.

As if she was trying to let him down easily, Cynthia responded, "Yes, and I know the team is forever grateful for your leadership. That said, I have been attending these meetings since you implemented 'Author vs. Editor' with your team and began rotating ownership, or as you put it, 'Authorship' of the meetings amongst the group. And some amazing things have taken place. Rather than waiting for you to 'Author' everything in these meetings like they have in the past, the team is really stepping up and showing a lot more ownership and initiative."

Still not convinced, Carlos countered, "Well, that is great to hear. But it doesn't mean that I shouldn't attend the meetings. What if I just attend the meetings and stay largely silent?"

Cynthia considered Carlos' offer. It seemed like a fair request that he was making but given what she had observed with the team in recent weeks, it might actually do more harm than good for Carlos to reinsert himself back into the team dynamic. After taking a moment to craft her response, Cynthia continued, "I think your presence might actually derail this new dynamic that I have been noticing with the team. They are having the challenging conversations with each other that they historically either avoided or looked to you to resolve. And they are ending all of these meetings by saying, 'What can we agree on as a team that we can present to Carlos for him to Edit?' In other words, your effort to get this team to step into the 'Author' role as a collective group is working better than even I thought it would." With that Cynthia gave Carlos a playful reassuring wink.

Carlos knew Cynthia was right. His absence in the senior team's weekly status meetings was just supposed to be a one-month experiment, but given what Cynthia was observing, the team was more collaborative, more candid and held each other more accountable *without* him being present in the meeting. And while it stung a bit to not be needed in these meetings, Carlos knew it was the right direction for the team and for him.

As Carlos and Cynthia began discussing his calendar for the upcoming month, more and more of these "you aren't needed" situations kept popping up.

"The procurement team won't need you in the meeting with the suppliers. They have said that they want to only bring you in for the final decision after they have done all the negotiations and weighed all of their options…"

"While the sales team has appreciated your engagement with top customers, they have realized that it has created role confusion with the customer. They have requested that you not attend these meetings and if the customer reaches out to you directly, please refer them back to sales leadership…"

"The monthly alignment meetings that you have been attending between finance and marketing leadership have also requested that you pause your involvement. They want to find a way to 'Author' solutions that work without always relying on you to intercede and resolve their conflict for them."

Carlos just listened as one by one, meeting after meeting, he was being requested to *not* attend. When Cynthia finished her revisions of his calendar for the upcoming month, Carlos was averaging almost a full day of "found time" each week. Intellectually, Carlos knew that this was his teams' effort to help him move out from being "IN" the business and move into a role that was more "ON" the business. And as the CEO, he knew it was the right thing to do. But that didn't make it hurt any less. If Carlos was gut-level honest, he actually liked being "IN" the business every week. It was exciting. It was dynamic. And, most importantly, he felt needed. What was he going to do now with all of his time?

And then Carlos saw it. Right in the middle of the month was the upcoming quarterly board of directors meeting. While Carlos did not dread these meetings, they rarely went as hoped. The Board was made up of many successful leaders, and like any group of confident and successful leaders, the Board was not short on opinions. Carlos always left these meetings feeling like it went "off the rails," clutching a list of follow-up action items that the board had requested. While his Board was always very supportive, the peppering of questions felt more like an episode of "Shark Tank" than anything else.

For the first time in his tenure as CEO, Carlos actually had available time to properly prepare for this meeting. But what would that look like? What did he need to do differently?

"Cynthia, I need your help thinking through how I can lead the Board Meeting this month more effectively. These meetings never go as I intend, and I just know there has to be a better way."

Cynthia eyed the calendar and realized that they had just a few weeks to prepare. "Carlos, of course I'm happy to help. A good starting place for us is to discuss how you typically prepare for these meetings. What do you normally do?"

"Well, I typically bring in all of the current financials of the company, and after I provide a financial update on the business, then I pivot to update the Board on how we are tracking towards our key strategic objectives," Carlos finished and looked over at Cynthia. She was jotting notes as he spoke.

"And? Is there anything else?" Asked Cynthia.

"No, and it's at that point the discussion always takes an unexpected turn," replied Carlos.

"What do you mean?" Prodded Cynthia.

"Well, let's take the last meeting. After I reviewed solid progress on the strategic objectives, we ended up spending over an hour debating if our supply chain strategy needed to be a bigger priority, and if so, what was the value of making it a bigger priority. Nowhere in any of the documents that I presented did I even mention supply chain. But because one of our Board members had recently gone through this exercise of examining the strategic importance of supply chain with her company, she felt it would be beneficial to share their findings. That then kicked off an entirely unexpected conversation." Carlos was visibly frustrated as he concluded.

Cynthia jotted a few more notes down. "So, if I understand this right, you provided updates to the Board, but you didn't have anything 'Authored' that you wanted them to 'Edit.' You didn't have any particular recommendations or options that you were presenting for them to discuss. And in the absence of that, a member of the Board 'Authored' a recommendation based on her experiences and that then sparked the discussion." Cynthia paused to look at Carlos. He was taking in what she said, but it was starting to click.

"And, if I was to guess," Cynthia continued, "You ended up leaving these meetings with a list of follow-up action items that the Board has 'Authored' for you to work on. Yes?"

Carlos could have kicked himself. This whole time, he had not actually been Authoring to the Board. Rather, he was letting the Board take over that role, which they happily did. Providing updates is not the same as Authoring recommendations.

"You are absolutely right. I can't believe I didn't see it before. I haven't actually been 'Authoring' to the Board. And by not doing so, I have been creating the opportunity for them to take over that role. This is something that I am going to fix starting today." Carlos had a steeliness in his voice.

"Before we get started, I notice you have a retirement dinner for a Dr. Marilyn Cooper the week of the Board meeting. Tell me more about that," inquired Cynthia.

Two weeks later, Carlos was in his car, hastily making his way through evening rush hour traffic. He had just concluded a full day with the Board, and it couldn't have gone smoother. The simple act of bringing a few 'Authored' recommendations and discussion points served as focusing agents for the Board. Like typical meetings, there wasn't any lack of spirited debate. However, the difference was that Carlos had determined the areas for debate. He not only felt in control, but also, he felt incredibly productive. The Board addressed the issues that he wanted them to address and, as a result, Carlos had a much more focused list of action items that came from the meeting.

Carlos pulled into the front of the building that housed one of his favorite restaurants, FOOD 643. The valet came over to Carlos' door, and after some brief pleasantries, Carlos made his way into the building.

Carlos approached the all-too-familiar elevator to FOOD 643. Per usual, two attendees were stationed at the stand in front of the elevator.

"May I help you?" Offered the first attendee. "Yes, I'm here for Marilyn Cooper's retirement party," responded Carlos.

After Carlos provided his name and was checked off the list, he was ushered into the elevator. Once he arrived at the top floor and exited the elevator, he noticed that the entire restaurant had been reconfigured for the party. Almost every table was full of guests for this special event. Carlos was feeling a bit overwhelmed as to where to sit, when luckily a greeter approached him and promptly escorted Carlos to his seat.

To Carlos' surprise, he found himself sitting at the head table. Marisol was already sitting in the seat next to him when Carlos arrived at the table. She was in the middle of an animated conversation with Sonya Nyugen. Next to Sonya sat Cynthia listening in to their conversation. Once Carlos sat down, he whispered to Cynthia, "You could have told me that I was going to be sitting at the head table." He gave her a smirk.

Before Cynthia could respond, Sonya and Marisol paused their conversation as they realized that Carlos had just joined them.

"Carlos, it is so good to see you!" said Sonya. "I haven't seen you in the store in quite some time," she prodded playfully.

"Well, given you now have thirty locations, and you have just started launching an e-commerce fashion concierge business, I don't know how you'd find the time to make it into the store," Carlos said with a smile. "Congratulations, by the way. What an accomplishment," he added.

"Thank you. It has definitely been a journey. And, of course, I couldn't have done it without Marilyn's help," Sonya responded.

"Sonya, I see you have met my wonderful wife, Marisol. Have you had an opportunity to meet my amazing executive assistant, Cynthia?" Asked Carlos.

Sonya and Cynthia gave each other a smile as if to say to each other, *Should we tell him?* "Carlos, Cynthia has been one of my most loyal customers for the last ten years. She has a fantastic sense of style," concluded Sonya.

Carlos was about to ask Cynthia why she never told him, when Simon Black, the owner of FOOD 643 came to the table and sat down next to Carlos. Instead of wearing his crisp white chef uniform, Simon was in a sophisticated gray suit with a black shirt and tie. He clearly intended to be part of the event and not "work" the event. He hardly looked different than when Carlos first met him nearly two decades earlier other than the addition of several pronounced streaks of gray in Simon's hair.

"Carlos, my friend. It is so good to see you!" exclaimed Simon as he reached out to shake Carlos' hand.

"Simon, it is great to see you as well. I seem to be at the table with some real rock stars. I was just talking to Sonya about the incredible growth of her business, and then you sit down. So, tell us, were you at your restaurants in New York City, Las Vegas, or Los Angeles this week?" Carlos teasingly asked.

"Actually, I just came back from Melbourne. I'm planning my next expansion back home in Australia," replied Simon. "I've got a great group of leaders here in the states that are fantastic 'Authors' to me and 'Editors' with their teams. When you have that, growth is not only easy, but it's fun too," Simon said.

Just then, Marilyn arrived at the table. After a chorus of greetings and hugs, Marilyn sat down. As she was making her way around the table welcoming everyone and asking about their lives, she got to Carlos and Marisol.

"Carlos, I already know about your boring job as CEO," she said with a grin. "I'd rather hear about your family. How are the kids doing?" She asked.

Carlos looked over at Marisol as if to say, "Do you want to answer or should I?" Marisol took the cue and responded, "Thanks for asking, Marilyn. Rafael still has his IT consulting firm. He just hit one hundred employees and is struggling to keep the culture the way he wants it. We have regular 'Author/Editor' conversations with him. Sofia, as you know, finished her Doctorate degree a few years ago and just got promoted to Associate Professor. And Jose has been traveling around the country doing audio engineering for large Broadway productions. He just hired his first employees last year and is struggling to get out of the 'Author' seat, primarily because he loves what he does so much."

"Marisol, you forgot to add the most exciting part," added Carlos. "In addition to Rafael's two little girls and Sofia's little boy, we are expecting another grandchild this Spring," Carlos said with a big smile.

The dinner was exceptional, and the room was filled with laughter. One by one, guests would stand and offer a few words of thanks to

Marilyn and recount how Marilyn had impacted them during her forty years of teaching. Soon, it was time for Carlos. He stood and raised his glass.

"I want to tell the story of how Marilyn not only saved my career and my marriage but made me a better leader and parent in the process. It all started when I called her twenty years ago. Her response was simple, and yet it changed my life. She said to me, 'Carlos, you have an Author versus Editor problem.' No truer words had ever been spoken."

And Carlos shared the rest of the story...

How to Maintain an Author vs. Editor Mindset

Many years ago, I was in graduate school for my counseling degree. One of the classes that I took was "Family Therapy." It was a fascinating course, although I could argue that my classmates were just as interesting. (Some individuals choose advanced studies in therapy and psychology as a means of doing their own individual work.) One particular concept has stuck with me ever since that course. It is the idea that a family system is a lot like a play. Every member of the family plays a part. One family member might be the martyr. Another family member might be the rescuer. Then there is the overachiever or the victim. Regardless, all families have their play that they put on night after night. The show must go on. I'm sure as you think about your family of origin, you could easily identify the cast of characters and the roles that they play.

Here's where things get interesting. When a member of the "cast" decides that she or he is no longer willing to play their part (Ex: You decide you are no longer going to be the rescuer, martyr, victim, etc...), the rest of the family does not celebrate their personal growth and deep work that they surely had to do to get to this point. On the contrary. Members of the "cast" revolt and insist that you go back to playing your part. Afterall, how are they going to keep the show going if there is no longer a rescuer/martyr/victim, etc...?

This analogy absolutely applies to your Author/Editor journey. Not everyone is going to appreciate or encourage your new approach. Consider any the following possible "threats" to your Author and Editor shifts:

- **The resistors.** Addressed in previous chapters, to Author is to be vulnerable. Not all members of your team will happily go along with your shift. Be prepared for push-back from some when you attempt to foster "ownership, initiative, and critical thinking."
- **The boss who refuses to abdicate the Author seat.** Some leaders prefer sitting in the Author seat. Perhaps they like the feeling of control. Or maybe they just get a rush from being "close to the action." Regardless, these leaders may need some extra persuasion.
- **The team members that Author up AND down.** You may find success in getting your direct reports to Author to you. Congratulations. But watch closely. If they don't encourage the same shift with their teams, not only will you not be effective in shifting the culture, but you could end up getting your team member close to burn out as she or he insists on Authoring up AND down.
- **The team members, leaders, or you that fall back into bad habits under stress.** Stress can cause some of us to back track on

the progress that we have made in our shifts. The Hall of Fame baseball pitcher, Greg Maddux, had a perfect way of capturing this slip. When asked "What is the difference between a good pitcher and a great pitcher?" Greg replied that when under stress, the good pitchers tend to try to get out of trouble by throwing *harder*, typically resulting in walks, hit batters, and a general loss of command. However, when the great pitchers get in high stress situations, they have learned to throw *softer* instead. Greg Maddux was a master of keeping his composure in those situations, which is why some argue he is the greatest pitcher of all time.

You will likely encounter high stress situations that will threaten the Author/Editor progress that you have been making. Be vigilant and don't be tempted to "throw harder" (i.e., Author when you should be Editing) in an effort to feel like you are in more control.

The Author/Editor shift can be transformative for not just you, but your entire ecosystem. That said, it is a journey not a destination. Here are a few important best practices to keep it from slipping.

Best Practices for Maintaining an Author/Editor Culture

1. Share this concept with as many members of your ecosystem as possible. The wonderful thing about the Author/Editor concept is that it is incredibly sticky. Share the concept with your team, your peers, your leader, your children, etc. And once you have, you'll find it becomes a common language that you all use. (Ex: "Can you Author some recommendations for us to discuss in our next meeting? Would you prefer that I sit in the 'Author' seat or the 'Editor' seat for this discussion? Etc.)

2. Infuse the "seats" into how you conduct your meetings. Create an expectation that your direct reports ALWAYS bring you something to Edit during their one on ones with you. This way, it becomes a habit and norm that they then reinforce, and hopefully, require and teach to their teams.

3. Lead with questions, not answers. In meetings with your team, at the dinner table with your children, and in a variety of other settings, you will be tempted to jump in with an "answer," when you would be better served asking questions to promote "ownership, initiative, and critical thinking." Consider the following examples:

a. Ex: During a team meeting, it becomes apparent that a critical project is behind schedule. You are asked, "What do you think we should do?" Rather than answer with a directive, consider challenging the team to come up with solutions. ("Rather than sharing my perspective, let's spend the next 30 minutes brainstorming some ideas and alternatives as a group.").

b. Ex: You receive an email from a teacher of one of your high schoolers indicating that the student has several missing assignments, and if not submitted soon, the student runs the risk of failing the class. Rather than immediately grounding your child and Authoring their calendar for the next week, consider bringing it to their attention and requiring that they Author a solution to the issue. ("I just received an email from your teacher indicating that you have several outstanding assignments that need to be turned in. Are you aware of this? If so, how are you planning on approaching this to resolve the issue?")

4. Get creative in how you Author to your boss. If you are encountering a boss that refuses to relinquish the Author seat, consider getting creative in your Author approach. Consider including visuals, charts, graphs, quotes from customers, anything and everything that might draw their attention. Some leaders may want to see your recommendations prior to the meeting so they can think about it. Communicate "what's in it for them." My point is simple. If you get resistance the first time you try to Author to your leader, don't give up. Keep adjusting until you find just the right way to present them a "menu" that they will order off of.

Warnings and Traps that Could Threaten Your Author/Editor Efforts

Naturally, we don't live in a perfect world. Below are the common traps and excuses that I hear as people slip from their Author/Editor efforts. Be wary of the following:

> <u>Trap #1</u>: **"I don't have a full team. I need to cover the empty seats before I can move into an Editor role."** Odds are, this is you right now. In fact, I don't think there is one client that I'm currently working with who doesn't have at least one open position on his or her team. That said, while you may need to play "player/coach" for a short period, DO NOT shelve the Editor role. In fact, I would argue that you need that role now more than ever in order to encourage the rest of your team to elevate their performance. And there is no better way to do that than to actively encourage "ownership, initiative, and critical thinking."
>
> <u>Trap #2</u>: **"My team is already stretched thin."** I had a COO client that suffered from this trap. He was working 75-plus hours a week.

When I challenged him to shift some of that work to his team to Author, his response was that he felt awful doing that to them. In his words, they were already "stretched thin." I then shared this story with him. During the pandemic, my wife encouraged me to join Orange-Theory Fitness. If you aren't familiar, OTF is a high intensity interval training workout (HIIT for short). You wear a heart rate monitor with the goal of "optimizing" your heart rate and your calorie burn as you build strength, power, and endurance. It is safe to say that I died in my first eight classes. Apparently, I have nine lives because I'm still here.

One particular coach, Mirka, took a liking to me. To give you a little context, Mirka is originally from Eastern Europe. At approximately six feet tall, a tightly pulled blond ponytail and an Eastern European accent (she enjoyed saying to the class "Welcome victims"), she is an intimidating presence. If Mirka likes you, she shows it by pushing you to go harder. One particular day we had to do a set on the rower and then immediately exit the rower and do tricep extensions on one leg with weighted medicine balls. As we were all lining up to begin the tricep extensions, Mirka came over to me, removed my 12-pound medicine ball and replaced it with a 25-pound free weight. She looked me in the eye and said, "You're welcome." You see, she wasn't afraid to challenge me to lift heavier weights, because that is the only way any of us get stronger when we exercise. We have to challenge our bodies with something heavier.

I shared this story with my client, and he responded, "What if you began to struggle. Then what?" In fact, I did struggle with the heavier weight. Mirka noticed and quietly came over to me. She never removed the weight. Instead, she provided some coaching on how to manage the heavier weight and still accomplish the exercise.

Don't be afraid to give your team heavier weights. I see too many leaders that are figuratively "the strongest in the gym" while their team sits around and watches them lift. The best teams are all strong and pushing each other to get stronger.

Trap #3: "We allow team members to come to meetings without something prepared." This is a subtle trap. You institute Author/Editor with your teams, but you have the occasional team member who doesn't show up prepared. This may seem like not a big deal to you. This is a HUGE deal if you let it go unchecked. Don't continue the meeting if they are unprepared. At best, it is a waste of your valuable time. At worst, you end up Authoring for them in the meeting. Immediately, cancel the meeting and reschedule for a time when they can come prepared. No Authored materials = No meeting. Stay the course.

A Final Word

I have been teaching Author vs. Editor to my clients for nearly five years. And in every situation, it helped them recover their time, their impact, their influence, and, in many cases, their personal life. I wish all of these outcomes and many more for you.

The good news is that the process works. Every time. I wouldn't have written the book if I didn't have full confidence in the tools that I am providing you.

With this book in hand, you have everything you need to change your world for the better.

The rest, dear reader is up to you.

Reflection Questions for You from Chapter 8

- Have you encountered any of the "threats" outlined above (Ex: the resistor, the boss who refused to relinquish the Author role, etc.)?
- What is your plan for sharing the Author/Editor concept with others in your ecosystem (Ex: Direct reports, your leader, peers, family, etc.)?
- How can you be more intentional to infuse the "seats" into your regular one-on-one meetings with your direct reports?
- How good are you at leading with questions, in general? How can you stop yourself from Authoring an answer when you should be encouraging Authorship from others?
- What are creative Authorship approaches that you think might work when you approach your leader with an Authored solution? Do they need to see it prior to the meeting? Do they respond better to data? Stories? Visuals? Etc.
- How can you avoid delaying sitting in the Editor seat until you have a full team?
- How can you think differently about giving work to your team so that you are encouraging them to "lift heavier weights?"
- How can you keep yourself and others accountable so that if a direct report shows up to a meeting without anything prepared, you have the confidence to reschedule the meeting on the spot?

Review Inquiry

Hey, it's Brandon here.

I hope you've enjoyed the book, finding it both useful and fun. I have a favor to ask you.

Would you consider giving it a rating wherever you bought the book? Online book stores are more likely to promote a book when they feel good about its content, and reader reviews are a great barometer for a book's quality.

So please go to the website of wherever you bought the book, search for my name and the book title, and leave a review. If able, perhaps consider adding a picture of you holding the book. That increases the likelihood your review will be accepted!

Many thanks in advance,

Brandon

Will You Share the Love?

Get this book for a friend, associate, or family member!

If you have found this book valuable and know others who would find it useful, please consider buying them a copy as a gift. Special bulk discounts are available if you would like your whole team or organization to benefit from reading this. Just visit www.theworkplacetherapist.com or contact Brandon directly at brandon@theworkplacetherapist.com for more information.

In addition, if you're interested, autographed copies can also be purchased for an additional nominal fee by ordering through the The Workplace Therapist website www.theworkplacetherapist.com.

Would You Like Brandon to Speak to Your Organization?

Book Brandon M. Smith Now!

Brandon accepts a limited number of speaking/coaching/training engagements each year and enjoys presenting in-person and virtually to groups from less than a dozen to 15,000 and more. To learn how you can bring his message to your group or organization, email him at brandon@theworkplacetherapist.com.

OTHER BOOKS BY BRANDON M. SMITH

The Hot Sauce Principle: How to Live & Lead in a World Where Everything is Urgent All the Time, Indie Books International, 2020.

About the Author

Brandon Smith is a leading expert in leadership communication and curer of workplace dysfunction. Known as "The Workplace Therapist," host of *The Workplace Therapist* podcast, and co-host of *The Leadership Foundry* podcast, Brandon is a sought-after executive coach, TEDx speaker, and award-winning instructor. He is the founder of The Worksmiths LLC, an executive coaching and leadership development firm whose clients include numerous Fortune 500 companies. Brandon has personally coached more than 1,000 leaders and executives across the globe, representing both for profit and not-for-profit organizations.

Brandon is also the co-founder of The Leadership Foundry LLC, a leadership development firm that works with organizations to create customized leadership development programs for their leaders, from frontline managers to senior executives.

In addition, Brandon is a highly requested keynote presenter and leadership educator. Brandon has delivered keynote presentations and leadership development sessions to over 100,000 participants over the last decade. As an adjunct faculty member at multiple prestigious business schools, he has won over a dozen teaching awards for his work in the classroom. Brandon has been interviewed by NPR, Fox News, the *Wall Street Journal*, NBC, *New York Post, Fast Company*, CNN, and many other media outlets for his expertise in leadership and workplace dynamics.

Brandon received an undergraduate degree from Vanderbilt University with a concentration in communications and team dynamics. His graduate work includes an MS in counseling from Georgia State University as well as an MBA from Emory University's Goizueta Business School.

He resides in Atlanta with his wife, their three children, and two loveable pups.

For information on executive coaching, leadership development, speaking, and other services, please contact Brandon at:
email: **brandon@theworksmiths.com**
Website: **www.theworksmiths.com**
Website: **www.myleadershipfoundry.com**

For additional resources by Brandon Smith on combating workplace dysfunction:
Website: **www.theworkplacetherapist.com**
Podcast: **"The Workplace Therapist Show"** — available on iTunes and Stitcher
Podcast: **"The Leadership Foundry Podcast"** — available on iTunes and Stitcher
Youtube: **https://www.youtube.com/c/TheWorkplaceTherapist**
Youtube: **https://bit.ly/3MHcMPP**

Connect with Brandon on Social Media:

https://www.facebook.com/brandonsmithwpt

https://twitter.com/TheWPTherapist

https://www.instagram.com/thewptherapist/

https://www.linkedin.com/in/brandonsmithtwpt/

https://www.linkedin.com/company/my-leadership-foundry